Intro the Cross-Walk

Bic

John Smiley Publishing
Philadelphia

Published in the United States by John Smiley Publishing
PO Box 2062
Riverton, NJ 08077-2062
U.S.A.

smileypublishing@johnsmiley.com

The characters and events in this book are real, as recalled by the author, although the names of some of the principle characters have been changed to protect their identities.

Into the Cross-Walk

ISBN: 978-1-61274-030-0

Printed in the United States of America.

10 9 8 7 6 5 4 3 2 1

First Edition: October 2011

Dedicated to my wife, the love of my life. Hey, that rhymes!

Cover art by Jody Brownd
www.CaricaturesByJody.com

Back cover art by Sarah Chauvin

About the Author

I'm Bic. Well, actually, Bic is just my pen name. My real name is Mark Chauvin. I live in Texas. Ever been to Texas? It's big. It's hot. It's also really, really flat. I've got four wonderful kids and a beautiful wife. I work on computers, I play bass guitar, I like to tinker with cars. I'm nothing special in this world. If it weren't for God in my life, I'd be a pretty pathetic loser. Now I'm just a mildly pathetic loser. Only by His grace does anything ever get done. I also believe in guardian angels; I don't know how anyone who remembers being a kid wouldn't. There are so many times I did something so stupid, and I should have died (I certainly deserved to) but didn't. When I get to Heaven, I want to shake that angel's hand (or wing or whatever) because he did a darn good job. After I'm gone, I can only pray that somehow I made someone's life a little better, or made a few people smile.

Introduction

Growing up in America can be a difficult experience. It's hard enough to figure out right from wrong without people trying to sway you one way or the other, but when you're out of the house & on your own for the first time, and you meet other people who are just as explosively free as you are, it's nearly impossible! The characters you meet and the stupid things you do during your late-teens are funny enough to be in a book, if they don't kill you first. I don't recommend ANYONE follow my path to maturity, however; there are many ways to get wisdom, and perhaps the most foolish technique is the trial and error method that I used. It's a miracle I'm still alive, and I'm almost sure I sustained brain damage & hearing loss from the experience. At least, that's what I think someone said to me once, but I don't remember if I heard him clearly.

In these pages you will find the story of my life, an average shmuck who's looking for that special formula to make life meaningful. In a very haphazard way, I explored the different avenues to fulfillment, or perhaps more exactly, I willingly responded to the blow of the wind. It cost me several years of my life, my only chance at education, my relationship with my parents and my formerly acute senses, but it is my belief that God himself had a plan for my life, and I was just thick-sculled enough to need those times to learn how wrong my choices could be. In the end, He directed me to Himself, and I've never been the same since...

Part I

Chapter 1: In the Beginning

I started out as a little cell in a warm, wet place. It was very dark. Don't remember much, either. Actually, my memory is kind of vague until age 18….

Chapter 2:   College

BangBangBangBangBang

BangBangBangBangBang

Ughumphpth? Whazzatt noiz?

BangBangBangBangBang

BangBangBangBangBang

Oi, my hed. What time is it anyway?

Geez, 7:30am. Those guys are never late.

I look out the window. There they are, 6 floors down. A half-dozen hard-hats wandering around. One of them is shaking in rhythm with the BangBangBangBangBang. Must be a jackhammer. The university decided to tear up a perfectly good piece of concrete. Why? To replace it with new concrete. Why? Well, I'm told that if you're a university, and you DON'T spend all the money Texas gives you to maintain yourself, then NEXT year they'll give you even LESS. So when there's money left over, you hire 6 hard hats and a jackhammer, and tell them to destroy the sidewalk next to the dorm. Makes sense to me.

I was never a very good morning person. Back at home, I used to hate getting up for school. "Mark, it's time to get up!" Why are mothers always so cheerful? "Mark, you'll be late for school!" Oh, thanks for reminding me. School. Now that's a pleasant thought to get you going in the morning. Always smiling, my mom was. Never figured that out. How could anyone smile so early in the morning. My dad was even worse. "Good morning, Son!" I still remember his bright eyes and silly smile. Made me want to puke.

But now I don't have an annoying mother to wake me. Instead, I get construction noises. So what class do I have to get to. Physics. Oh boy. I love physics. Nothing like a little physics in the morning. And how nice that I got up at 7:30. I might miss my wonderful physics class, which starts in only ... 3 ½ hours.

Since you can't really sleep next to a jackhammer too well, I decide to visit the local misery cafe. The dorm's cafeteria serves a wonderful assortment of stale bread, old cereal, scrambled mammal eggs (they're reputed to be from chickens, but you'd never guess that by their appearance) and various condiments left-over from the war. I decide like I always do on a bowl of Captain Crunch and milk. Bet my parents would love to find out I'm spending their meal ticket on synthetic food substitute. It's a wonder that I ever grew tall.

Eventually, I make my way to class. It's a bit of a walk; the University of Texas is a big campus. I'm awash in a sea of people. Nobody notices me.

Nobody cares. There's the sorority self-indulged rich girls, bouncing happily next to their built-like-a-tank-with-just-as-much-brains boyfriends, a multitude of very serious-looking white guys with glasses, and a surprising number of Oriental Rambo's. If you've never been to college before, these guys are going to take over the world. They're smarter than you, they work harder than you do, they LOVE going to class, very serious, and they always carry a programmable, scientific calculator in their holster. Some of them even speak English.

In class, I find a seat near the back. Or I guess you could say near the top. It's one of my smaller classes – no more than one or two hundred. Gosh, you should see my chemistry class! I never did find out what my instructor looked like. All I saw was a dressed pink figure with a brown spot on top, which I assumed was his hair.

Being so gleeful and awake, I had lots of energy to spend on this class.

"OK let's say we have car, and it sitting still. We give gas, and it accelerate 35 feet per second per second."

Why am I taking this class again? My eyes wander around the room. Everybody else is paying attention.

"Then train A is falling at 32 feet per second per second to train at Pittsburg..."

I vaguely remember my dad telling me to go to college. I didn't know what I wanted to be when I grew up. I still don't. But he was an engineer. My brother was in college to be an engineer. So, here I am. Becoming an engineer.

"So you add speed of train to glass of water and give gas to pour out..."

Did you ever hear of that guy who got up in the University of Texas clock tower with a rifle & killed a bunch of people? I would never do that, but if I did, I think this guy would be my first target.

"So the two train exert force on fly, which make three liters per second falling ..."

Somehow this isn't making sense. I mean, here I am, potentially the world's greatest bass player, and I'm spending all my time learning how fast rocks fall! I mean, maybe that can be useful to me, like, I can calculate how fast the raw meat is going to fall that I throw at my screaming fans someday, but who cares? Life is too short.

"And you get 3.7. Ok, have we test tomorrow. Goodbye you later."

I think they hire these guys to teach the class from some foreign embassy or something. "I'm sorry, but you speak good English. We don't have any openings right now." I manage to stay awake long enough to get back out in the good ole' Texas heat, then I go back to the dorm for a nap. I haven't uttered two words since I woke up. Good news! The vibrating hardhat is on lunch break, and my roommate is gone. Time for a little snooze.....

Chapter 3:   Josh and the Jesus Freak

"Who's JOSH?"

"Come see what Josh has to say!"

"Josh will tell you how to LIVE!"

It was all over the campus. Written in the sidewalk with chalk, on posters nailed to power poles, taped to doors & windows. This guy "Josh" was some big-shot Christian speaker & was going to speak for two nights at the student theater. Being a good Catholic but rather naive about who's a Catholic and who isn't, I decided this would be a good thing to go to. As it turns out, I was free that Thursday anyway. So I went.

The lobby was full of lively, young students smiling and handing out the programs. "Hi! Glad you could make it! Enjoy the show!" I grunted behind my glasses and messy long hair. I hate cheerful people. Makes me want to slap 'em. These are the kind of people that are happy all the time, even when they're sick. "Hi, doctor! I'm constipated!" "Well, I think you need an enema." "OK! Let's get started!"

I pick a nice seat in the shadows and wait. Not many people here. Most of the crowd is smiling, too, like a giggling child with a secret. A few of us unsuspecting slobs in the back grew a little uneasy, I think, like you do when you dress up for a wedding and then go to McDonald's for lunch. I just didn't feel like I fit in very well there. Oh, well. I was safe. I'd just watch this Josh guy for a little bit, then leave if I didn't like it. Nobody's going to fetch me onstage or put me on the spot – no problem.

"Ladies and gentlemen, I'd like to thank you all for coming out tonight. Let me introduce our speaker to you, Mr. Josh McDowell." She goes on to list all the reasons why this guy is the most wonderful person in the world. More knowledgeable than God Himself and works twice as hard as Mother Theresa. Can't wait to see him. "And now I give you, Josh!"

Josh waves as he strolls across the stage, smiling as he motions the happy crowd to silence. "Hello everybody! I'm glad you came out tonight. Tonight I'm going to tell you something that can change your life, completely, and the best part is, it's totally free!" Well, that's a good start. I can have something very valuable for free. I know how that works. Like the free toy in the Cracker Jacks. It's only free if you shoplift.

"If you just ask Jesus to come into your life, and change you from the inside out, I promise, in six weeks you won't even recognize yourself!" OK, I can relate to this. I knew all about Jesus. He was Mary's son, or God's son, or both. I didn't know he actually DID anything. Figured he just sat upstairs playing God. "I'll tell you a little story. There was this young man who came to me & said, Josh, I just don't have any happiness in my life. I mean, I've got it all – a good job, a nice car, tons of money, lots of friends. But

9

I'm just not happy." (My response would be, 'You're an idiot! Be happy!') Josh continues, "So I told him, Friend, what you need is some real change. All those things are outside; you need help from the inside out. What you need is Jesus Christ. So we prayed this prayer, and I saw him about six weeks later. Josh, he tells me, I'm a new man. I quit drinking. I quit going to bars and smoking dope." And NOW you're happy? "I'm truly happy for the first time in my life. And Friend, let me tell you, the same thing can happen to you. All those things in your life – drinking, partying, drugs, music – can't make you happy. There's just one way to be happy, and that's with Jesus Christ."

Well, there goes that theory. I've been in church all my life, and I still get depressed.

He goes on & on with examples of people who turn from murderers and pimps and drunkards into perfect little people that never frown or do anything wrong, all because of this little prayer.

"OK, now I'm going to say this prayer. I want everyone here to close their eyes while I say this." Just like church. Bow your head, close your eyes, try to stay awake. "Dear Jesus. I know I can't be happy without you. I know you're the only one who can really change me. I'm asking you right now to come into my heart, and change me from the inside out. Amen."

I open my eyes. Everything got real quiet.

"Now, I know a lot of you folks out there said that prayer with me. And if you did, I'm telling you, in six weeks you won't recognize yourself. Jesus will change you, make you into a new person. You'll be truly happy for the first time in your life." OK. I kinda said that prayer with him. Yeah, yeah I DID say that prayer.

"Thank you for coming tonight, and please bring a friend with you tomorrow, when I'm going to be teaching on MAXIMUM SEX!" He goes off stage, everybody claps politely, except for the people from the lobby; they're down on the front standing & cheering like crazy. One of them gets up to basically tell us "It's over. Go home." She used nicer words than that, though, but I wasn't listening.

All the way back to the dorm, I'm thinking about that prayer. I say it again, just to be sure I get it. "Jesus, please change me. I'm not happy with the person I am. I want to be better." That should do it. If Josh was right, I'll be totally different in just a month and a half. I didn't know how, but I figured, what could it hurt?

The next night, the place is packed. (I wonder why.) Josh spends the first hour or so talking about how you shouldn't have sex until you're married. "Sex is only one twelfth of a relationship, but what a one-twelfth!" So, if I ever get married (HA!) and I want better sex, there's eleven other things I have to do first. Yeah, right. Knew there had to be a catch. Actually, there's eleven catches. Blah blah blah...

Everybody loves having an adult up there using words their parents never did. He mentions the M word, the S word, talks about lust & what men want & what women want. Pretty juicy stuff for a grown-up. Then Josh changes gears & closes his show. "Now, if you were here yesterday, I told you if you said this prayer, then in six weeks you're not going to recognize yourself. All you have to do is ask Jesus to come into your life, and change you from the inside out. I want everyone to close your eyes while I pray..." He goes through the same song & dance as before, and THIS time I'm sure to pray with him. I don't know how many other people did, but after that night, I knew something was going to happen. In just six weeks.

~~~~~~~~~~~~~~~~~

I'm staring at my poster. It's a picture of a beach with footprints on it. No people; just footprints. I saw it at a store in the mall with my parents once, and I liked it, so I bought it. Had a poem on it. Went something like this:

I died. I looked behind me. Footprints. Sometimes two sets, sometimes one. When my life stunk, only one set. So I asked Jesus. Where were you? He says, I didn't leave. I carried you. The end.

<sniffle> Touching, isn't it? I love that poem.

Anyway, so I'm looking at this poster. It's the only God-type thing I have in my half of the dorm room. I'm thinking, it's been 8 weeks. I gave you two extra weeks, and I'm still the same person. It didn't work. I don't understand.

It was late. I was bored, and a little disappointed, so I went for a walk. I used to walk all over that campus. In the middle of the night, when about 39,900 of the 40,000 students are gone or in bed, you can actually think, it's so quiet. And as long as you stay on campus, you're pretty safe. The campus cops are always riding around pointing their lights on you & asking for ID. They sure do a good job.

So being the immature bone-head that I was, I left the relative safety of university property and wandered off to this little park by the college. It's wonderful what the Austin guys can do to a ditch. Put some brick in here, a bridge there, a few tables & Voila! it's a river walk. Very pretty. Nicest ditch I ever saw. I'm walking around, thinking & enjoying the silence, when I notice someone ahead of me. I think I recognize him; it's one of those guys that was telling us about Jesus. Said his life was changed, said the prayer, and kaboom! He was a different person. What's he doing up at 2am? So I decide to stalk him – eh, follow him.

I catch up to where he's reaching into a trash can to get an old newspaper.

"Hi." Guess I said that a little louder than I had to.

He seems surprised to see me. He jerks upright & drops the paper back in the trash as he whips around to see who it is.

"You remember me? We were talking about Jesus the other day."

"Oh, yeah, I remember." A sense of relief & familiarity crosses his face. "What's up?"

It's hard for me to open up so quick, but I respected this guy. I mean, he was older than me! Besides, he seemed to be happy, and I wanted to be happy too. "Well, I wanted to ask you a question. You said Jesus changed your life."

"Yes, He did," he said with a smile.

"Well, is there any reason why someone would pray & ask Jesus to change them, and it wouldn't work?"

"Gosh, I can't imagine that."

"Because I did that, but I don't feel any different."

"I don't know. It worked for me. I can't imagine it wouldn't work for you."

This guy seemed happy, all right. I was beginning to see why. No brain, no pain.

I had another question. "Do you believe in hell?"

"Oh, yes." His smile never changed. "But God's too good to leave people in there forever."

"Really? Don't bad people need to be punished, like Hitler?"

"Oh, I'm sure Hitler's out by now. In fact, he's probably walking around and you don't even know it's him."

I wonder if he believes in Elvis, too.

"Well, thanks. I guess I'll see you around."

"OK, good-bye." He turns back to the trash-can, picks out the newspaper & starts reading it.

I left the park with a bit of an empty feeling. Jesus didn't want to change me. I was probably not worth saving. And the one person I knew of who had changed was completely brain-dead. Maybe that's it. You have to be stupid to be happy. Maybe I'll take a bunch of drugs & give myself brain damage; THEN I'll be happy.

Just before I passed over the hill, I glanced back at him. There he was, bent over his free newspaper, reading in the darkness. The light from the lamppost gave his hair a shimmering gold glow in the darkness. If ever I saw one, THAT was a Jesus Freak.

Chapter 4:   Meet the Girl

Crash is my best friend. He's getting an engineering degree, too, but that's just for fun. What he really does is play guitar! We make a good team. He plays guitar, I play bass, we don't have a drummer, or a singer, or a sound system, but darnit, we KNOW we're good! If we can play Judas Priest, we can do anything!

The one big problem we had in college was being 19. We could drink if we wanted to! Hooray! No more standing outside the 7-11 asking strangers to "do us a favor". No more snitching the parents' Vodka & refilling it with water. No more sneaking off from my grandmother's house in Louisiana to buy whiskey where you only have to be 18. This is cool! Unfortunately, we each had a roommate, and it wasn't each other. Finding a place to drink was just as hard as it used to be to BUY the stuff.

One time, we got this wonderful bottle of wine. Only five bucks for a half gallon! What a bargain that was. We decided to drink it in the parking lot there of the convenience store. Didn't take us long. I used to be able to chug down a 32-ounce super big gulp in about 60 seconds. We finished it before we had walked to the road, which is about how long it took for me to start throwing up.

"Hey, Mark, pretty good stuff, eh?" He hits my shoulder. He didn't hit it that hard. But for some reason I just kept going backwards, & backwards, & backwards... I know I must've fallen down, but I couldn't feel it. Then when I stood up, I felt something else. Uh-oh.

BLEAH! BLEAH! BLEAH!

That was fun. Spend five bucks to throw up in a parking lot. To this day I can't drink more than a teaspoon of wine at a time.

Instead of using a parking lot, the next time we decided we needed to have a better place to drink our beer. After all, it wasn't just any beer – it was Grolsch! Crash had some German blood in him I guess, and I guess I did too, because this stuff was GOOD! But he didn't want to bother his roommate again, and I didn't have a fridge, so we decided to take it somewhere & drink it. We wandered through campus (it was late), and after the campus police told us not to consume alcohol on university property, we decided to take it to the student union.

Only one problem. No bottle opener. Us college guys didn't have money for luxuries like that.

We were dejected, wishing we could drink our warm German beer in peace, when all of a sudden these two girls came up to our table.

"Hi, guys! Mind if we sit here?"

Heck, no. They were actually girls! Sure, one is a short, stubby little midget and the other one weighs more than both of us put together, but you can't be too picky when it comes to girls. Besides, it would be rude to say no. So we both say "Sure!"

"What's your name?" asks the Large One.

"Mark. What's yours?"

"Dino. You're cool. Let's buy some beer."

"Hi, I'm Dorothy," chimed in her smiling little friend.

"Hi. This is Crash," I offer.

"Hello." Crash is polite but always, always cool. "Let's have some beer."

We weren't about to tell them we brought a six-pack of warm Grolsch with us, but we didn't have a bottle-opener. It was under the table, where it was going to stay for awhile.

"I'll go get us some." I come back with four big ones. Dino takes hers and engages me in some highly intelligent conversation.

"You guys are cool. Everybody else here is so nerdy."

"Really?"

"Yeah. You want to go to a concert or something? You should call me tomorrow."

"Uh, well, I guess I could."

"Promise?"

"Well...."

"Promise?"

"How about some more beer?"

I'm going broke, but it's worth it. A slight kink in the evening is when someone at the bar mistakes me for a girl. I turn around. "I'm not a girl."

"Oh."

"I guess you got confused because of the long hair."

"Yeah, I did. Bet that happens a lot to you, doesn't it?"

Back at the table with the fat chick and her miniature sidekick. Jumbo has attached herself to my left side, clamping my arm with her free hand as the other one hoists the fresh mug of booze to her lips. Her long hair brushes against my face as she throws her head back in laughter at one of our stupid jokes. Oohh, I like. At my diminutive weight of 140 pounds, we must have seemed a lovely couple. Ever seen an elephant dating a stick bug?

"Call me tomorrow? Promise?"

"Ok"

"Promise?"

"OK"

It was starting to sound like a better idea the longer I sat there drinking beer. Hey, she didn't seem so fat now. Actually, she was lookin' kinda good. I thought her friend would be perfect for Crash. Unfortunately, they weren't hitting it off as well as me and Dino were.

"So, you play guitar?"

"Yeah, I do."

"My brother plays guitar."

"That's cool."

He kept looking at me. He was smiling, but something in his eyes said, "You want me to get that giant leach off of you?" Them two never did get together. Guess he doesn't have the same animal magnetism that I have. Wonder why I'd never charmed a female before then? Guess I'd never met the right girl...

We walked around; the girls went home. Turns out they were staying in the girl's dorm across campus. We said goodbye, and walked off in our swaying, cool, "I'm cool - are you cool? I know I am" walk. Little did I know what a role that girl would play in my life. I think she ended up calling me the very next morning. She even beat the hardhats out of bed.

Chapter 5:   Trouble in Paradise

"Let's go for a walk."

"Sure," I agreed. This was great! I was in college, away from my parents, and I met a girl who thinks I'm really cool! Ah, freedom is so sweet. Sure, I hated my classes, I couldn't sleep late because of the hardhats, I stayed out really, really late with Dino, I hadn't studied for days, or even practice my bass playing for that matter. Come to think of it, all I had been doing for the last few weeks was Dino. Dino, Dino, Dino. Hmmm.

"Let's go down the Drag."

"All right." The 'Drag' was Guadalupe Street, the main street in Austin by the campus. It's where all the really cool people hang out. There's an ice cream shop, a mall, record store, some book stores, and a rock-N-roll shop, which is a great place to buy all kinds of weird stuff that I guess rock-N-roll people like. Knifes, incense, drug paraphernalia. I guess that's so you can get stoned, kill someone & smell good all at the same time. And then there's the people. Mostly college kids, and Drag Worms. Drag Worms are people who dropped out of college there & live on the streets now. They look at you with bloodshot eyes, kind of swaying back & forth as they clutch their little brown bag & say, "Got any change, buddy?" And there's always a pretty girl or two to look at.

WHACK!

"Hey, what was that for?"

"You were looking at her!" Dino seemed upset.

"Looking at who?"

"That little redhead over there! You like her, don't you?"

Well, I thought, let me check her out. Hmmm. Not bad. Long hair, shapely hips, high heels.

"No. I didn't even notice her."

WHACK!

"Ow!"

"You're such a liar. I'm going to have to put blinders on you so you can't look at anyone else but me." I couldn't tell at first if she was kidding. She packed quite a punch, but I was no wimp. I could handle a little abuse. I think she might have been serious.

This kind of hurt my ego a little bit. So just to affirm my manhood, I put my arm around her.

"Stop that."

"Stop what?"

"I don't like it when you touch me in public."

OK. No problem. I can handle that. I'll touch you later, then, right? I pull my arm back.

"Let's go back to the dorm," she says.

"OK." My enthusiasm was starting to go down a little. And my arm hurt. "I need to study anyway."

"No, I've got this really cool new album, you want to hear it?"

"Well, I've got this test tomorrow..."

"Come on, you'll get an A. You're so smart. Besides, I thought you didn't like that class. Wouldn't you rather be with me?"

OK, think hard. Alone with Dino, or alone with a physics book. Dino, or book. Dino, or book.

"OK. Let's go to the dorm." It wasn't rocket science. I could study later.

Well, later never came. I stayed out late, then a little later, then finally got back in bed right before the hardhats got to work. I woke up with a headache. The phone rings.

"Hi! It's Dino!"

I manage a weak "Hello."

"I'm coming over in a few minutes. You want to go somewhere?"

"I have class in a few hours. I have to study for that test."

"Oh, come on. You can study for that test later. Let's go do something."

I got out of bed, got dressed, & met Ms. Morning Person in the lobby.

"So, how about some breakfast? You want go to the cafeteria with me?" My weak eyes hadn't reached their fully open position, but I could make out her broad smile in the piercing sunlight.

"OK." Sure. Whatever you say is fine with me.

The day progressed pretty well. I took the test. I think I flunked it. Dino was waiting for me when class was over.

"So, how did it go?"

"I think I failed."

"No, you didn't! I'm sure you did great. You're so smart. You want to see a movie?"

"Not really." I can't focus on anything anymore. I'm so tired I can't lift my arms. I look like a gorilla with my hands dragging the ground, except I have longer hair and better breath.

WHACK!

"Ow. What was that for?"

"Oh, yeah, checkin' out the blonde, are you?"

"No." Was I? Maybe it was an automatic response. Maybe the gorilla in me was coming out. "What blonde?"

"That one over there."

Hey, she's kind of cute.

WHACK!

"You WERE looking at her!"

"Dino," I groaned.

"How come you keep looking at other people? Don't you love me?"

"Uh, yeah..." I never really thought about it before. Did I?

"You're going to go off and marry a slinky redhead, aren't you?" She was especially wary of girls with red hair. Probably because I told her I had a fetish for redheads. (Guys, never do that. Repeat after me: I have always wanted a girl just like you; I have always wanted a girl just like you.)

"No, of course not. I'm not going to marry anyone." She didn't seem to like that answer very much, but she didn't say anything. "Let's go to my place," I suggest.

"OK"

We walk two miles uphill in the snow during an avalanche in the middle of a hurricane on bare feet over broken glass to get to the dorm. Or so it seemed. I was exhausted. I open the door. My roommate's gone.

"Mind if I listen to some music?" Dino asks with bouncy excitement.

"Sure, go ahead. I'll be back in a minute."

Don't know why, but I felt like I needed to call my mom. I lumbered down to the lobby & picked up a pay phone.

"Collect call from Mark," I breathed into the phone. I can hear it ring at my parent's house as I lean against the booth with my eyes shut.

"Hello?"

"Collect call from Mark, will you pay?" How do the operators do that? No emotion or anything. Wonder if they have to go to school for classes like Nasal Voice 101, or Beginner's Monotone. Or if they have to try out for the part. No, I'm sorry, you can't be an operator with a voice like that. I can still tell you're human.

"Mom," I said. The rest of the words wouldn't come out.

"Mark, what's wrong?" Why'd she have to say that? Moms can tell when you're hurting. I can feel a lump rising in my throat. I can't talk. "Mark, what is it? You can tell me."

"It's ... I ... well, I met this girl, and she keeps wanting me to do things & go places ..." I'm choking back tears. "I ... just can't ..."

"Oh, honey, you can't let her do that to you! She's using you!" She sure hit that nail on the head. And quick, too.

"Well, it's just, I'm always tired, and she's always calling me & wants to do stuff. <sniff>"

"Well, you can't let her do that to you! She's taking advantage of you! You're your own person, you need your space!"

"But I can't just tell her to leave!"

"Sure you can! Tell her you just need a little time, that's all. Just tell her your mom said you need a little rest. OK, honey?" That sounded like a reasonable idea. That's not rude at all – I'll just tell her I need some space.

"OK, Mom. I think I will." It felt wonderful to have someone on my side. Even if it was my mom.

"Are you going to be OK, sweetheart? You want me to come up there?" Mom asks with concern.

"No, I'm all right. I'm just going to tell her I need a little space, that's all."

"OK, honey, take care of yourself. I love you."

"I love you too, Mom." I hang up the phone, and check the lobby to make sure no one can see me. Some tough guy I turned out to be. Crying on the phone to my mommy.

This is OK. I'll just tell her I need some space. That's right. Space. It's no big deal. I can do this. It's just too much. I need a break.

The elevator dings & I walk over to door. Be strong, Mark. Dino's waiting for me on my bed, smiling and sitting Indian-style under my giant Rush concert poster. I avoid her eyes.

"I just wanted to tell you, I think we've been spending too much time together. I need a little space." I decide it's a good time to wash my hands in the sink.

"WHAT? Who have you been talking to?" What is it with women? They read me like a book.

"My mom." I tried to make it sound nonchalant. No big deal. Gee, I better scrub that finger. It looks dirty.

"So how long do you 'need space'?" she asked with a touch of sarcasm.

"Just a couple of weeks." Sounded reasonable to me. I was really, really tired. I stole a glance at her.

The best way I can describe her is like someone who's getting ready to blow up a big, big balloon. She's taking a deep breath, eyes wide & focused, face a little red, intent on not only blowing that balloon to full size, but busting it open so fast she'll knock a hole in the wall from force of the explosion.

"I can't believe you said that, after all I've done for you! You remember the first night we met, and you said you'd call me? I didn't even go to sleep that night. I waited all night long for morning to come, and I called you as soon as I could. I can't believe you want more time to yourself. You must not even care about me. I can't even sleep. I want to be with you every minute. That's how love is. When you love someone, you want to be with them. Fine." She comes up for more air. "You want to be alone, I'll leave you alone. But don't try calling me any time soon. Jerk!"

She storms out of the room. "Dino! Wait."

"You just don't care about me. What'd your mother say, 'she's using you?' You're such a jerk. Go talk to your mommy."

"Dino..." I was mad, too. I couldn't explain why, but something didn't seem fair. She's yelling at me, and I didn't do anything wrong, did I? Dino heads down the stair well, slamming the door behind her. I open it up & yell down "Dino, wait!"

"Forget it!" She's a few floors down by now. I stand at the top wondering what to do. All of a sudden, I feel a stinging sense of injustice about the whole situation.

"<Slang expletive for female breeding canine>!" I slam the door, kind of surprised that I said that. Maybe she didn't hear me. But I meant it. To heck with her. Mom was right. She WAS using me, and all I wanted was a little space.

Crash came over later & we had a little snack. OK, so it wasn't a snack, it was Vodka & Coca-Cola. The dorm hall was busy. It was Friday, and there were people everywhere. I was upset, and I needed a release.

"Hi, guys, how are y'all doin'?" A couple of girls came over to say hi. Crash was smiling at 'em.

"Just fine. How are y'all doin'?" he said, as he peered out between his curly black hair locks that draped his face. Crash was cool. He always knew what to say.

"I think I'll get a little drink," I said. I didn't know what to think. I liked having girls in my room, even if they only came over to see who the weirdo's standing in the hall were. But I didn't want anything to do with girls. I figured they were all looking for a personal punching bag or a victim to torture with sleep deprivation and guilt.

I got out a nice clean – uh, a nice, uh, glass, & filled it up with coke about an inch or two, and added the rest with Vodka.

"Oh, my god, did you see what he just did? Look." She seemed kinda cute. She took my glass. "He filled this up with about this much coke, and THIS much Vodka!" Pretty impressive, isn't it?

I didn't care. I didn't want to feel anything. I didn't even want to taste it. I chugged it down to comments like "All right, man!", "Go!" and a girlish "Wow!"

"Hey, Crash," I say. "Let's play some music. How about that Accept song? You know, the one I like. 'Balls to the wall'." What a fine musical masterpiece that was. So profound and meaningful. I can still here that chorus: 'You've got your balls to the wall, man... Balls to the wall.... You've got your balls to the wall, man ... Balls to the wall'.

"You know, this radio isn't very loud," Crash commented

"Hey, let's see if we can make it louder." I had an idea. I had a bass amp. I had a musical-instrument 15" 200-watt ElectroVoice EVM-15B high-efficiency speaker. I had a cable that could go from the boom box to the amp.... If I connected this here and plugged it in here and turned on the song...

"YOU'VE GOT YOUR BALLS TO THE WALL, MAN... BALLS TO THE WALL...." It was great. We stood at the doorway & grinned. Everyone was looking our way to see where that beautiful sound was coming from. I actually hadn't ever heard anything that loud before. I stood in the doorway & I could feel it shaking.

"Wow, that is LOUD!" Crash was impressed.

The hall monitor wasn't. He's the guy that's supposed to make sure everyone behaves on our floor. "You need to turn the music down!"

"What?"

"I said, you need to turn the music down! It's too loud!"

"Oh, OK, after this song, all right?" He shakes his head & walks off, a little irritated. I never ever saw that guy mad. He was so cool.

"BALLS TO THE WALL, MAN! BALLS TO THE WALL!"

Someone came up from downstairs. "Your music is too loud!"

24

"What?"

"I said your music is too loud!"

"We're going to turn it down after this song."

"I can hear it all the way downstairs."

"What floor?"

"The first floor!" We were on sixth. That must've been a record.

"Wow, cool!"

"So you'll turn it down?"

"What?"

"I said, YOU'LL TURN IT DOWN?!"

"Yeah, sure, right after this song!"

"BALLS TO THE WALL, MAN! BALLS TO THE WAAAAAAALL....." After a final crash of the drums, the song was over. I turned it down, as promised. For some reason, it didn't sound so good any more. Maybe it was the Vodka, or maybe I had ruptured my ear drum. (Actually, the next day, I found out I blew the speaker. Not an easy thing to do – that speaker was built like a tank!)

The next thing I remember is waking up in my dorm room with a massive headache. "Good morning. How are you feeling?" That was Tom, my roommate. He was a nice guy. I knew he wasn't yelling at me, but it sure felt like he was.

"My head hurts." I slowly roll out of bed. Why is the floor moving around?

"You're not sick any more?"

"Sick? Was I sick?"

"Yeah. Looks like you threw up on the floor, then you tried to throw up in the sink. There's also some throw up in the hall. I went ahead and cleaned it up."

"Thanks." I don't remember that. Well, maybe I do. It's kind of blurry. I went to the bathroom & noticed a couple more puddles of regurgitated Vodka, & tried to clean it up as best I could. I was in a lot of pain. It hurt to stoop over.

Back in the room, I sat down. What did I do last night? Oh, yeah. Had a fight with Dino. Then I drank some Vodka & played a song through my amp. I never noticed how bright the sun was. I'm SO glad the hardhats are off today.

RING! The phone is especially loud and painful today.

"Hello?"

"Hi, son. It's me, Dad."

"Hi, Dad." It hurt to talk. Even more than it hurt to breathe or open my eyes. "Where are you?"

"I'm downstairs. Can I come see you?" Huh? Doesn't he live in Houston? I'm in Austin. Mom must've told him I was upset. He drove all that way just to see me?

"No, just stay there, I'll be down in a minute." I tried to remember. Did I talk to him last night? Did I call my mom back & like threaten suicide or something? Why was he here? I went down to meet him.

"Hi, son!" Ouch. Don't yell so loud.

"Hi, Dad. What are you doing here?"

"Well, Mom told me you were having some trouble, so I came up to see if I could help you out. Have you eaten yet?" Actually, food sounded pretty good to me. And I was very, very thirsty.

"Sure."

"Do you know a good place to eat? My treat." OK, this isn't so bad. As long as he's paying, let's get something good.

"How about Schloski's?" It's a sandwich shop. I usually never went there. Too darn expensive.

We talk. We eat. Boy, I'm thirsty. Dad buys me a super-size Sprite, and I buy a refill for 25 cents. I tell him about Dino & he tells me Mom was right, she's using me, I need my space, blah blah blah. Gosh, I was thirsty. I pause for a moment outside the restaurant.

"I don't feel so good." I feel something sloshing around in my innards.

"Why, does your stomach hurt?"

"Yeah. I think I'm going to throw up."

"OK, well, let's try to find a bathroom. Maybe there's one in this place."

We go into the video arcade and my dad asks the guy at the counter, "Do you have a bathroom?"

BLEAH! It just came out. Yuk – sprite and chunks of sandwich meat all over the floor and the front of the counter. The guy looks up from his book. "No, but I wish I did." Without another word, he hands us a roll of paper towels & goes back to his book.

I'm never going to drink again. I feel terrible. It's embarrassing. Here I am, a college student, and a future world-famous musician, and I'm in a video arcade, cleaning up vomit off the floor with my dad on my hands and knees.

It was sure nice of my dad to drive all that way to come see me. After we soaked up my former stomach contents with about a hundred paper towels, he walked me back to the dorm. He can see I'm not at my peak so after wishing me well & pledging his undying support, I make a slow, careful ascent to my room for a little nap.

Later that evening, I'm feeling much better. I walk over to meet Dino where she works on the Drag. She'd be getting off about now.

"Hi!" I give her a bright cheerful smile.

No response. She just looks at me, scowls and turns away.

"What's wrong?"

"You don't remember, do you?"

Remember? Remember what? Oh, that's right. I wanted more space. Oops.

"I changed my mind. I don't need any space. Want me to walk you home?"

She gives me a look that seemed to say, 'I'll think about forgiving you, maybe', gets her bag & we start walking.

Out on the sidewalk we start talking. "You got really drunk last night."

"Yeah, I know," I said with a chuckle. How did she know? Was she there?

"I came back to see you, and you were passed out. Crash said you drank a lot of Vodka."

"Yeah, I did." Actually, I'll have to trust Crash on that one. "How much did Crash say I drank?"

"A liter. I called the pharmacy to ask him what to do. He said to keep shaking you & if you respond, it'll be ok. I stayed there about 2 hours, then I let you sleep." Gosh. A whole liter! It's a wonder I didn't get alcohol poisoning and die. Good ole' George (my guardian angel). Always on the job. Dino looks over and scowls at me. "You told me a whole bunch of stuff in your 'devil voice', like you hated me and you think I'm too pushy. Do you remember any of that?"

Now that she mentions it, I do remember. I guess the Vodka allowed me to open up a little. That 'devil voice' was part of a song I wrote – it's really cool. Something about going to school, and lockers covered with blood – I forget the rest.

"I'm sorry, Dino." I tried to be sincere, but still sound cool. I'm not sure that I was sorry, exactly.

"It's OK, I guess." And that was that. Everything was back to normal. She still hit me when a pretty girl walked by, and I still spent every waking moment with her. But I did manage to secure a little dignity for myself.

After all, it's not everyone who can blow a 200-watt speaker and guzzle a whole bottle of Vodka in the same night, and live to tell about it!

Chapter 6:   A Name for a Band

Heavy metal. Just say that again, slowly. Hheeaavvyy mmeettaall. Savor the way it rolls of your tongue. Admire its tone and timber. Know that there is no finer, no better form of musical expression on Earth. Mozart was an idiot. Beethoven was clueless. Now, Metallica, or Motorhead – THAT was real talent!

I was first introduced to heavy metal music via a high school friend of mine, Jim. Jim was a nice guy. I was a nice little nerd with straight-A's in 9th grade, and he taught how to slouch, wear dark clothes, talk about people behind their back & basically disrespect everyone. He also gave me a musical appreciation for early heavy-metal pioneers like Kiss and Jimi Hendrix. He had moved away, but we kept in touch. He wrote me once & mentioned he liked some song or other because it was real "heavy metal." So, I went to the local record store & asked for the heaviest metal they had, & sent it to him on his birthday.

"Whoa, Mark, what IS this stuff?" he wrote me. "Where'd you get this? This stuff is awesome! This band makes KISS sound like a bunch of wimps!"

After that, I had to hear it for myself, so I bought an album & I was hooked. In case you're not familiar with this particular genre of music, let me give you a little introduction. If it sounds loud at any volume, the guitars sound like they're giving birth to octuplets, the drums sound like they're being pummeled by King Kong, and the lead singer can hit notes higher than a chipmunk undergoing electro-shock, it's heavy metal. And if you see the musicians, and you're scared thinking about running into them in some dark alley, and you can't see their eyes for all the hair and they're wearing at least 90% black, it's heavy metal. And if you see someone listening to it, and he looks like a kid who just got expelled for selling drugs or smashing the principle's windshield or maybe stuffing a dead cat into a cheerleader's locker, and it's hard to hear yourself think it's so loud, and you start having thoughts of violence and rebellion and total mayhem, it's heavy metal.

My particular taste in music was in the purest form of heavy metal; raw and non-commercialized. You'd never hear bands like Titan or Slayer on the radio. Speed metal is what I called it. I figured, if a band slows down, I turn it off. The absolute, best band I've ever heard was called Watch Tower. And no, they're not associated at all with the Jehovah Witnesses. They had a drummer that could blow Neal Peart away, and a guitar player that went so fast I think he had to fireproof his guitar neck. Now, the bass player was what I really liked. I've never heard anyone play as good as he did, ever. It's a shame guys like that have to stay in small-time bands like Watch Tower. He had long hair, played without a pick, and moved all OVER that fret board. Man, he was awesome.

We used to go see them in Austin. We'd go down to 6th street to a place called the Ritz. It was only a few bucks to get in. One time, before college, we made the trip just to see Watch Tower. They'd be jammin' away on stage, with Jason the lead singer throwing his hair around like a rag doll having a seizure. It'd be so loud you could feel your chest move three inches with each bass note. We'd listen, slam dance, listen, slam dance. Those guys in Austin were crazy. The local concerts in Houston had freaks that stood there, smoked their funny-looking cigarettes & pounded the air with their fist while yelling "All right!". But in Austin, the group by the stage would thrash about, slamming into each other, pushing, shoving, all while banging their heads around. People would get on stage, thrash their head around & pretend to play guitar, then run out & JUMP on top of the crowd. You'd get an elbow in your ribs, a boot in your neck, people would fall onto you. It was fun. By the end of the evening, we were sore from head to toe, and our ears rang, but we were still glowing from having brushed with greatness. What a band!

We tried to play like Watch Tower, but in the beginning, the best we could do is try to imitate some of the tamer bands, like Judas Priest. It was just me & Crash. Crash bought a mail-order guitar from Carvin, and I bought a 4-string Ibanez bass my high school senior year from the music store. We played together at his house, talking about how we were going to be really famous some day. But we needed a name. What were we going to call the world's next legendary heavy metal band?

Fresh from our first semester at college, over Christmas break we were discussing a few options. I came up with a couple of ideas. "How about 'The Thrashers?' Or 'The Trashers?'"

"Nah, I don't like those," Crash said. "Maybe we could be called 'The Brothers of Hell' or 'Death Death Death.'" That last one sounded pretty good. I don't think the name's been used yet, except there is a band called MegaDeath (they aren't very good).

"Let's go for a walk & maybe we'll think of something," I said. It was early – probably not even midnight yet. We put our gear down & made our way over towards the elementary school.

We were walking through the soccer field, when I noticed a car driving down the street that we had just crossed. A big old car, maybe a cutlass or something, and the exhaust was smoking pretty bad. The guy looked like he wasn't paying very good attention to what he was doing. His tires rubbed against the curb, he ignored the stop sign & made a big u-turn before stopping next to the soccer field. After the cloud of exhaust cleared away, I thought I could see him stagger out & head our way. I didn't care. We saw all kinds of people when we walked around at night. Besides, we had an important issue to resolve.

"How about the, uh, The Killers? Or, Metal Death?" Crash's ideas were pretty good, but we needed a great name, not a good one.

"Or the, uh, Crazies? Or The Scream Team?" I thought that was an awfully good try. I mean, it rhymed. It's hard to think of words that rhyme.

We reached the playground & were sitting on the monkey bars. Crash looked thoughtful. "How about the, uh, the uh..." He straightens up a bit & says with a smile, "That's it! We'll be called Theuh. Thea!"

Brilliant! That was great! What an awesome name. Thea. Sounded gothic, or medieval or something. "Cool. I like it." I can just see the headlines now: 'Thea goes platinum!' 'Tonight at the Astrodome: Thea in concert for 6 nights! (sorry, all sold out).' 'Thea music blamed in death of 3 teachers!'

We were walking back to Crash's house for some more practice, when that guy from the car sees us. He's big, he's black, and he can't walk straight.

"How you boys doin' tonight?"

"Uh, fine, cool. How are you?" Hope the guy can't tell I'm a little nervous. I mean, he was big, and his eyes were all red. For a second, I think, maybe this isn't a good idea, meeting a big drunk black guy in the middle of the night, behind the school where no one can see us.

"Oh, I'm OK." He sounded harmless enough. His voice was low and raspy (probably too many cigarettes) but he almost sort of smiled. "My car stopped working back there. I think it has a dead battery."

Crash pipes up, "You need any help? I think my dad has some jumper cables." Crash always cared about people. He was a real humanitarian.

Mr. Big Black Guy turns to Crash. "Nah, it's cool. I leave it for a few minutes, it'll charge up. What are you boys doin' out here so late?" So late and all alone, I think to myself.

"Aw, we're just hangin' around, talkin'." I didn't want to tell this guy about the band idea. He didn't look like the kind that would appreciate fine music like we did.

"I know what you doin'. I seen boys like you all over the place. I killed bunch of you's too. You think you're cool, you're smokin' dope & stealin' cars. Probably dropped out of school too, huh?" Uh, excuse me? What was that bit about killin'?

Crash shoots me a glance. "No, we don't do any of that. We don't steal or anything." What is this guy? Some sort of vigilante? Goes around killin' teenagers? "And we're still in school, too," he added.

Mr. Black sways back to the right & looks at me, more or less. "That true? I know how you guys are. You think you're all cool, don't want no school, don't want nobody tellin' you nothin'. You got it all figured out. Well, let me tell you somethin'. I dropped outta school, I didn't think I needed to know nothin', I got me a job, and now I really got nothin'. You boys need to get your little asses back in school and make somethin' of yourselfs. You got a future, know what I mean? Are you hearin' me?"

"Actually, we're both going to school at the University of Texas," Crash says. I notice he's talking kind of loud & slow for some reason. "We're electrical engineering majors. We're just on Christmas break."

"Yeah," I add intelligently.

The guy looks kind of surprised. "No kiddin'? No way, you guys are in college?" Guess he doesn't see too many long-haired smart kids hanging out in black concert jersey's behind the school at 1am. Go figure.

"Yeah, we both go to college," Crash affirms. Crash is getting a little more relaxed, and shifts his weight and puts his hand on his back pocket. The Big Man's eyes follow his motion.

"Don't do that, man. I know what you're doin'. You got some kinda blade back there in your pocket. You don't wanna do that, I'm tellin' ya," he warns. I'm thinking, listen to the man, Crash. The last thing you want is this crazy guy thinking you're about to attack him.

"I don't have a knife in my pocket," Crash says very matter-of-factly. Doesn't seem concerned at all. "And I don't think you have to go to college to become a good person. There's lots of ways to learn about life. I mean, do you think the only way to become smart and successful is to get a college degree?" Crash the philosopher. Good job, Crash. This is a perfect guy to have an intellectual argument with.

"I'm tellin' ya, y'all need to quit what you're doin', and get back in school. If you don't do nothin', you won't get nothin'." Crash reaches up to scratch his nose, then puts his hand back on his pocket. Mr. Crazy gets a little more agitated. "I told you, leave you knife in your pocket! You gonna get hurt thata way."

"I told you, I don't have a knife in my pocket." Crash is amazing. Most people would be just trying to get rid of this guy. Crash wants to raise his blood pressure some more. "I know what you're saying, but what about other countries? What about places where people are poor and they can't go to college?"

"I said, you don't do nothin', you won't get nothin'," says Mr. Blood Pressure. He's staring Crash in the eye now, poised like he's ready to jump on him & squeeze his throat to the size of a toothpick any instant.

"Yeah, I know, but I think there's a lot of different ways for someone to get an education. Like, the Hindu's on the mountaintops. They go talk to the guru, and he's not at the college. They probably know more than we do."

"I'm tellin' ya, you don't do nothin, you don't get nothin'!" He pauses for a moment & looks a little thoughtful. "Why haven't I killed you guys yet?" Crash leans over onto the other leg. "You askin' for trouble, with that knife, boy."

"But I told you, I don't have a knife." Crash is totally unconcerned that he's about to be turned into flesh pâté.

I can't take any more of this. "Crash, he's trying to say, if you don't do nothin', you won't get nothin'!"

Mr. Killyou looks over at me. "Yeah, that's what I'm sayin'." He nods approvingly. "Glad at least one of yous understands. All right, then." He's not the only one that's relieved. Whew, that was tense. Crash looks annoyed at me.

"Well, I bet my battery's charged up by now, so I'll be leavin' you boys. Have a nice life, and stay in school!" And with that, he turns & stumbles off towards his car again. He stops a few paces later & turns back towards us. "I know what y'all are sayin', there goes one crazy nigger, but you listen to me, I know what I'm talkin' about. Y'all have a good life, now." With a wave of his hand, he turns back around & disappears in the darkness. Me & Crash look at each other.

"That was weird," I comment.

"Yeah, it was," Crash replies. Neither one of us say anything for a minute or two.

"So, we got a name for the band, eh? Thea," I say cheerfully.

Crash's expression brightens up. "Yeah, Thea. Cool."

We walk back to his house for more practice & chit chat. The car is gone from the street by the soccer field. I'm not thinking about the crazy black guy anymore. My mind is on my future. I'm sure we'll make it big; really, really big. It's just a matter of time.

Later that night, after my parents were in bed, I called Dino and told her the whole story. She got mad at me over the incident with the Black Murdering Drunk. "I can't trust you to be alone over there. I can't wait until next semester starts. I need to keep an eye on you. Don't walk around at night any more!"

"Uh... OK." I didn't know what to say. She totally ignored the news about a name for the greatest musical group to ever walk the earth. Just wanted to have me around so she could control me & take care of me. I didn't know anything about girls. I just figured they were all like that, you know, concerned about their man, worried about his safety, wanting to put him in a cage and tie him down for his own good, and manipulate him and never let him out of their site. I think what she really wanted was to be with me

24/7, making sure I never went out at night or did anything dangerous or saw or (God forbid!) talked to another female ever.

I was beginning to loathe the idea of being tied down. But, as it turns out, Dino got her wish, just like she always did.

Chapter 7:   Let's Live Together

I don't know if you'd call Dino a real "catch". I found out she had just broke up with her boyfriend and had been date-raped twice in the past week before I'd met her. (Never trust a drummer. They just want to bang on things.) But she liked me, and that was enough to take my mind completely off school. Not that it was focused too well to begin with, of course, but I like to blame it on her. Besides, I could die any time & then I would have wasted four years of my precious life learning about how fast rocks fall. There's so much that's more important than school.

She was constantly pressing me to do something I knew a good Catholic boy shouldn't do. It's amazing what kind of excuses you can come up with. "God, I know I'm not supposed to do this, except in marriage, but um ... I'm going to marry this girl. Yeah, that's it, I'm going to marry her someday, so this is really like my wife, we just haven't had the ceremony yet. Actually, I haven't even thought of it until now, but it sounds like a good idea ... I'll ask her later." I wasn't fooling anybody.

Somehow, I managed to make it through my classes that first semester. The pressure didn't let up after Christmas break. Pretty soon she's saying, "Let's get an apartment together." I know what that means – free sex! Any time, any day, whenever I want; like a contract. Why else would she want to live together? I'll do this if you do that. She was always kind of pushy. From the "Promise you'll call me. Promise? Promise?" in the student union to the "Come on, don't you love me? There's nothing wrong with it" and now the "Let's get an apartment. I found one real cheap. Let's go look at it" talk. Did I mention that I spent half my savings talking to her on the phone over Christmas break? That wasn't good enough, either. I ended up flying to Dallas to see her at her parent's place, the day after I had four wisdom teeth pulled. My parents thought I was crazy. Must've been quite a site, this hippy on the plane with a bag of ice on his face, probably smelling terrible. (At 19, I still hadn't developed my sense of smell; that's a common problem with teenagers.) I guess you'll do anything if you're in "Luv".

The apartment was a real gem. It had a swimming pool. I never saw any people in it, but rumor has it that it was 6 feet deep at one end, although you couldn't see the bottom through the thick green paste. I take that back, I did see someone in it once. I heard a splash, and I looked out from the balcony to see the landlady dragging her chocking daughter out of the muck. She was OK, but it's a good thing her mom was right there. Otherwise, you'd never find her in that dark pit.

I have a thing about roaches. My mom swears she never had roaches, but me & my brother & sister know better. We knew if you went into a dark kitchen, you reached WAAAY over & flipped the light on, and then you jumped back and carefully looked around for the large, oblong shapes scurrying around. If it looked clear, and you wanted silverware, you would pull the drawer out about an inch & slam it shut. That gave the roaches time to escape before you got your fork out. Every once in awhile you'd find a brave roach (or stupid) and it'd scare you to death when you open the drawer back up. I've had nightmares because of the times roaches have crawled up on my legs or flown across the room. There is nothing worse in the world than a flying roach. And these are not the little beetle-size ones you see in some places: these were a full two inches long, with wings and big antennas. I've often thought, you know, if God had filled up Hell with roaches instead of fire, I bet a lot more people would think harder about being sent there. All you'd have to say to me is, See here, Mark, it says 'And he cast the sinners into the lake of roaches, where they are tormented day and night by having Texas roaches crawl all over them & fly around', and I'd be ready to do anything. Where do I sign? What can I do? I don't want to go there! NOOOOOOOOOO!!!!!

But fortunately, the roaches we had in our wonderful little apartment were not the giant ones I knew and hated in Houston. They were only about an inch long, and brown. But what they lacked in size they made up for in quantity. I'd go to the bathroom and have to knock them off the pot first. The dead ones would form a mass grave underneath the fridge every week or two. Once I picked up a pot plant to water it, and there were a couple dozen parallel-parked underneath, making a solid mass you couldn't see through. Sometimes, I'd wake up to having one on my face or crawling across the sheets of our bed (well, mattress – who can afford beds?).

One day we met this guy at the pizza place. He was an exterminator, and he was hired to kill the roaches in the area. We made friends, and he gave us a good deal for coming over to rid us of our brown roommates. He sprayed this stuff in the doors, through cracks, on the floor. I think he used up about four cans. His last comment was, You may not want to stay here tonight.

Holy camoly! Those guys were everywhere! On the walls, on the floor, on the ceiling. In fact, it was raining roaches – the ones on the ceiling were getting sick and losing their grip. It was awful. I don't know how we survived. And remember, this is an apartment that supposedly exterminated once a month. (What'd they use, sugar water?) Our cat was having a blast. A real cute cat named "Spike." She liked to chase 'em around & chew their heads off. Then she'd come over & meow for attention with roach legs stuck to her face. Yech! Go away!

Chapter 8:   Mr. Dean

"The dean will see you now."

I shouldn't say I was nervous, because I really wasn't. I hadn't attended classes in about two months. Pretty sure my grades weren't too hot. I made a decision to spend all my time with Dino and play guitar & work at the pizza joint, because those things were SO much more important than a college education. For some reason, I never even thought about how I was spending my dad's college money making F's. In fact, I forgot to mention my decision to him at all. Silly me.

"Mr. Chauvin, sit down." When you're in college, you don't get any respect. People tell you what to do, where to sit, and they act irritated if you show any emotion. The "Mr." was just their way of saying "total stranger with a last name of Chauvin". I sat down.

Sometimes you have to marvel at the human body. How can such a worn-out person still make it to work every day? The skin is sunken, the circles under the eyes make the eyes themselves look like little peas. Hair now is a side ornament, like garnish on a plate, just a little to "dress up" the head. I'm glad he didn't smile. Probably cause a heart attack.

He's looking over a paper, which I think is my "I want out of college" request. That's a form you fill out with your name, social security number, phone number & reason for quitting. I think I put "want to be a rock star" in that blank. He sits there so long I'm afraid he's gone into a rigid coma. But then he moves an eyebrow & looks at me with those two little peas.

"Mr. Chauvin," (there it is again) "are you sure you want to drop out of school?"

No, I was just kidding. What I really wanted was to invite you to play football with some of the guys...

"Well, it's just not important to me right now. I've got other things that I want to do." Yeah, like go back among the living.

Mr. Dean takes a long look at me and then stares back at the paper. His eyebrows move down in a frown – hey, I never noticed that. He's got more hair above his eyes than on his head...

"I see that you've been on the honor roll."

"Yes, sir." I figure, it won't hurt to be nice. I didn't really care if he approved my application or not. So what if I get all zero's and pull my grade point average down to 2.0. How often do you think Eddie Van Halen has to give up a gig because his "permanent record" has an F on it? But it WOULD be kind of nice if I could keep my A's on my record, just in case the band thing doesn't work out. Nah – it will. I'll be famous, and I'll be riding in limo's and I'll have a huge bass amp and I'll grow my thumbnail real long and have hair down to my ankles and...

"Why did you wait so long to fill out this application?" Mr. Dean looks at me right in the eye. Ever stared death in the face before? <shudder!>

"Well, I've been busy. I've got a job at the pizza place." Bet that impressed him! I wasn't some pitiful college kid who didn't know how to get a job. No, sir! I'm not riding on my Daddy's coattails. I don't just sit around and learn from books – I drive a pizza truck! I'm a success!

A long time passes.

A long time.

A really, really long time.

Have you ever wanted to watch a pig decompose? How exciting that must be...

"Well, I suppose I'll approve it." Whoa – really? That's good news. Now if I ever decide to be a nerd again (HA!) I'll be able to come back here & re-take my physics class. Can't wait to meet Mr. Give Gas Falling Rock Train Pittsburg again. After another couple of eternities, he managed to sign his name to the bottom & hand the paper back to me. I take it gently from him & say good-bye. He doesn't react. Wonder if he knows I'm going to be the next Michael Jackson. Wonder if he knows who Michael Jackson is.

"Thanks. See ya." My command of the English language is impressive isn't it?

Out back in the sunshine! What a great day this is going to be. First, I'll walk over to my apartment (<giggle> I have an 'Apartment'), then I'll eat, then I'll go to work...

Life was good.

Chapter 9: A Job, a Friend and a Sore Fist

After me & Dino decided to live together & I quit school, I had to get a job. I'd only had a couple of jobs before. I mowed lawns when I was a kid, and I worked at Taco Bell for awhile. Mowing lawns was almost fun, except for the heat. It'd be 98 degrees outside, with humidity of 90%, and there's Mark, pushing a lawn mower around or sweeping the sidewalk. You couldn't find another kid outside for miles. I could only do one lawn per day. I'd spend the rest of the afternoon under the ceiling fan with a cold drink. I also worked at a grocery store once, but that doesn't count. I was very young and my job consisted of cleaning the gunk out of the shelves (the slot where the price stickers go) with a toothpick & wiping down the egg shelves. Compared to mowing lawns & scraping raw egg ooze, Taco Bell was easy. Sure, it was a lot of pressure, people complaining about their food & everybody in a hurry, but at least I didn't have to sweat.

So I looked for something in the fast food industry, and ended up landing a job at Pantera's Pizza. It was within walking distance of my new Roach Mansion, and the pay was real good, like maybe $4 an hour! Plus, you got tips from people on deliveries. The first person to train me was Michael Scott. He's where I got my driving skills from.

"So, this your first time in a pizza truck?"

"Yeah." I was a little nervous, but not much. I mean, new job, all on my own, don't know anybody there. So far I had acquainted myself with the broom and the dough-maker. Now it was time for me to go on a few deliveries.

Michael Scott started the little truck's engine & pulled out towards the street. "Well, we've only got a couple of pizza's to deliver. One's downtown and the other one's on 19th street." From what little I knew about Austin geography at the time, downtown and 19th street were pretty far apart. "We'll have to kindof hurry."

Just then my neck is popped back as the screeching tires launch us out into the main road. "Hang on," is all Michael Scott said. I caught a blur of landscape fly by my window as I pull my head forward.

"Wow, you always drive like this?"

Michael Scott swerves into the next lane to avoid a parked car. "Well, you have to get the pizza's delivered in a decent amount of time. Don't worry. I haven't been in an accident in awhile." He makes a hard left onto Congress, where I can see the capitol building quickly growing larger in front of us. "I think I know a shortcut." Silly me. I thought those alleys were for people, not cars. We finally grind to a halt in the street next to an office building. "Let's go." We're in the street, all right, double-parked in the right lane. We walk up to this little office building with a glass door, and Michael Scott takes the pizza over to the front desk.

"That'll be 6.50, madam," he says politely. I'm just standing there, like an idiot, still trying to catch my breath. The business woman at the front desk takes the pizza & reaches in her purse.

"Here you go. Keep the change," she says. Michael Scott says "Thank you," pockets the cash & whips around back to the truck.

"How much did you get?" I ask.

"About a buck."

"Is that pretty normal?"

"Yeah, it's OK. Sometimes you get a bigger tip from, like, parties & stuff." Hey, an extra buck per pizza can really add up, especially if you deliver them at warp 10.

Michael Scott taught me a lot about driving that day. Stuff like, use your instincts, rely on your reflexes, the road belongs to you, park anywhere, look out for cops. It was exhilarating. He slowed to only twice the speed limit on the way back.

"So, Mark, are you in college?"

"No, in fact, I just dropped out. I'm moving in with my girlfriend tomorrow."

"Cool," he nodded. "I'd like to have a girlfriend. You know, I don't like 'em too skinny. I don't like 'em fat, either. I like 'em thick. Thick, with long hair." That's weird. He just described Dino. Of course, everybody has their own idea of what 'thick' is. The crust of the earth may seem thick, until you look at it in a science book. Looks thin as a piece of paper. "What's your girlfriend like?"

"Well, she's real pretty, and 'thick', not too fat," I said. "She has really long hair, too." I didn't pause to consider the wisdom in telling this to Michael Scott, the guy who just told me he's looking for a girlfriend that's just like mine. "Maybe you can meet her some day," I offer stupidly.

"Sure, that'd be cool." It's hard to tell what he's thinking behind those dark glasses. Telling him about Dino turned out to be a really bad idea.

A few days later, Dino meets me at the pizza joint & Michael Scott is there.

"Michael Scott, this is Dino. Dino, this is Michael Scott."

Michael Scott comes over & bows. "How do you do, madam? I must say, you're looking ever so lovely today." He takes her hand and kisses it. "Pleased to meet you. I am Michael Scott."

Grrrrrrrrr.

"Hi, I'm Dino." Dino seems amused, which kind of irritated me a little. Maybe I should slap her, like she slaps me all the time. Then again, she's thicker than I am...

"May I join you?" Michael Scott asks. He's got that coy confident drooling look of his on.

"Sure," was Dino's response. Not exactly what I'd hope she'd say.

We sit. We talk. Michael Scott never looks at me the whole time. He feeds her a bunch of bull about how he's got this secret experiment on plants going on in Alaska, and he used to fly jets for Russia, all kinds of garbage. He either made it all up, or he's Superman.

"Let's go back to my place, and I'll show you some of my best work." Yeah, I bet you'd like that. "Let's all go & just chill out for a while." He looks at me for the first time, which is good, because I thought he forgot I was there. Dino is smiling.

"OK, sure. I want to see just how much bull you can come up with."

Grrrrrrrrr.

So we walk back to his place, which is just a block away from the Roach Mansion, and we sit, listen to music, talk. He says something, I don't remember what, something about a band she likes, but Dino jokingly points a finger at his face & says "Hey, that's one of my favorite bands!"

Michael Scott says with a smile, "You know what you're supposed to do when someone points a finger at your face?" And he licks her finger. Actually, he almost swallows it. I don't know about you, but someone swallowing your girlfriend's finger is a little past the boundary of simple friendship. Maybe I should leave so they can go a little further. Dino only smiles back.

Grrrrrrrrrr.

I finally get Dino out of there & we walk home. It's very, very late.

"Michael Scott really likes you," I comment, trying not to sound accusing.

"Oh, he's funny," she replies. "I don't even take him seriously. He's just kind of cute, that's all. You're not jealous, are you?"

Come on, now, if I even share a sidewalk with a pretty girl, I get a bruise on the arm, and you're over there letting him lick your finger? "No, I'm not jealous," I lie. Who could be jealous of him? I mean, he's hitting on my girl, and my girl is encouraging him, and the guy lives a block away and works the same place I do, so he'll probably see her all the time, and she's just the kind of girl he wants, and apparently doesn't care that we're kind of attached, but jealous? Me?

Us three spent a lot of time together. Somehow it just happened, over the next few weeks. It really starts to bother me. So outside the 7-11 one evening I say, "Michael Scott, I've got something to tell you. If you don't keep your hands off my girl, I'm going to rip your lungs out." I tried to be polite as possible.

Michael Scott reaches over and puts his arm around Dino. "Mark, I want you to know, I would never do anything to take this lovely, beautiful creature away from you. You have absolutely nothing to worry about from me, friend."

Grrrrrrrrrr.

Take your #*@#$&!@# arm away, and maybe I won't have to break it, I think to myself. But because I'm a peace-loving hippie, (and NOT because I'm a wimp, because I'm not, I'm not a wimp, I'm not, I'm not), I do nothing. Absolutely nothing. Except brood a little. Dino thinks the whole thing is funny.

A few days later, we're having another fight. Me and Dino, that is. They're getting really common. I didn't do something she wanted me to do, I think, and she couldn't understand why I was making such a big deal over it, just do it, and I didn't want to because I felt like she was always telling me what to do, and she says it's just my silly male ego, etc. etc. etc. I ended up saying, "fine. I'll just leave. Guess you don't want me around here anyway." I was getting good at pushing her buttons. I knew just what to say to make her mad. And leaving was the ultimate, because now she had no chance of winning the argument.

I was headed down the stairs & out to the street when I heard this CRASH! coming from my apartment. What the heck was that? I thought about going back to see what it was, but I figured she must have broken the window. I figured she probably threw my bass at it, because she HATED it when I practiced, but later I found out she just hit it with her fist.

I was too mad to see if she was OK, and I was definitely too proud to go back after walking out. So, I spent all night walking around, thinking. I walked all around the frat houses & sororities. I tried to walk on campus, but the campus cops kicked me off because I wasn't a student any more. "Visiting hours start at 10am." Gosh. Drop out and suddenly you're an outcast. Picky, picky. I got hungry, and I discovered that there's a lot of bushes around that have this kind of peach-looking fruit on it, and it was pretty good. Sure, it might have been poisonous, I didn't know, but at that point I was wishing I was dead anyway. I knew I would be when I got back to the apartment.

During the night, on a hunch, I decided to walk by Michael Scott's place. I went up to the door & listened. I could hear someone inside talking to Michael Scott. Sounded like Dino.

"And he always says ... but I can't ... then he ..." It was hard to make out the words. I could hear Michael Scott replying in a tone that seemed to say, "I know how you feel, what a jerk, you're such a good person, it's all his fault, let me give you a hug..." I couldn't stand it any more. I heard all I needed to hear.

I spent the rest of the night getting angrier & angrier, but I didn't go back to the apartment. When I finally did go back in the morning, Dino was there & we had a little chat.

"So, did you have a nice walk?" Dino's voice still had an edge to it.

"Yeah, I guess so." I was tired. I should have just slugged her for cheating on me, but I'm a peace-loving wimp – I mean, hippie. Let's cut to the chase. "Did you go over to Michael Scott's place last night?" I watched her for a reaction. I expected surprise and maybe guilt, but not from Dino. She was too tough to show weaknesses like that.

"Yes, I did. I went over there to talk to him because you were being such a jerk." That's it. When you're accused, don't defend yourself – attack! "Nothing happened, if that's what you're worried about." Her voice had a condescending tone to it, like she was talking to a spoiled child.

"Well, I'm tired. I'm going to bed," I said.

"That's fine. I was just leaving." Dino grabbed her purse & walked out without a hello or sorry or anything. I sat on the couch and talked to myself about how I should have said this or should have said that. I think of these really great lines about 20 minutes after a fight. Lot of good it does me. I calmed down after an hour or so, and crashed. I was exhausted.

That's how it was for awhile. Tension you could feel. Icy words meant to hurt each other. Sarcasm at every opportunity. Eventually, we did get over it, but the fighting came back quite often.

Life was not fun with a mad Dino. Not fun at all. I still enjoyed being with her between fights, but the high I got from actually getting close to a girl was starting to wear off. Sometimes I had trouble reminding myself why we were together.

Chapter 10:   The Biker Guy

I make Dino out to be pretty bad, don't I? Well, she WAS pretty bad.
Before I met her, I thought all women were nice & sweet & cute. I owe
Dino for showing the evil, dark side of a woman to me. I can spot that in
other women now, too. They may seem nice on the outside, all caring &
talkative & loving. But you get them mad, or cross them in any way, and
POOF! out comes the black hat & broomstick. I think every woman in the
world has the capability of being a dark, evil witch, under the right
circumstances. Of course, for girls like Dino, that circumstance can be any
time the moon isn't full, or whenever the sun is shining somewhere on
Earth, or a certain time of the month, or two weeks before that time, or
during that time, or two weeks after that time.

And she was so controlling. I remember one time we were walking along,
going through Dobie mall to get a pizza from Nikki's, and this guy was
handing out flyers to anyone who would take one.

"Here you go, sir. Please read this." I automatically accepted the typed
sheet of paper.

I got to read the first couple of words – something like "Jesus wants" – and
the paper disappeared into thin air. Pretty spooky, huh? OK, so it didn't
disappear; Dino snatched it away from me, crumpled it up & tossed it in the
trash.

"Hey! I was going to read that!" I protested.

"You don't want to read that. It's just about religion." She held my arm a
little tighter as she strode towards Nikki's. She had a disgusted scowl on her
face, like some smelly drunk had just tried to grab her and she was trying to
walk away.

"I wanted to read that," I said. I went back to get another one. She
wheeled me around & said, "Come on, let's go. You don't want any of that.
Let's go get our pizza." And so I consented, and got a pizza. I never did
find out what that paper said.

But all this didn't seem to register on my puny little punk brain. Later that
afternoon, after yet another big fight, I went to meet Dino after she got off
work. She was with another fat chick – I mean, thick chick. That was
Andrea, from New York. Everything Andrea said or did was great, because
she was from New York. She was just as pushy & self-confident as Dino
was. I think Dino would have fit in well in New York.

"Hi, Dino," I said as she came down the steps to the street.

"Oh, hi. Andrea, this is Mark. He's my boyfriend." She seemed cheerful, if
a little distant. She could have paid me a little more notice than she did,

after our huge fight. I was kind of hoping for a makeup hug, or maybe some serious talk. Dino had other plans.

"Hi, Andrea. What are you guys doing?"

Dino answered, "We're going to the union for some drinks." She looks at Andrea. "I hear there's a really cool band there tonight." Andrea nods and they turn towards campus. Dino adds, "Oh, do you want to come?" as an afterthought.

"Well, am I invited?" was my reply. Dino looks at Andrea and gives her a knowing glance with a bit of a chuckle.

Andrea smiles & says, "I'm not getting into this. This is between you two." I get the impression that they've been talking about me. I also get the impression Dino is still ticked off. Well, so am I, dadgumit. To heck with Dino and her thick friend. I'm not going to be an afterthought for two fat chicks.

"Fine," I said, and turned around & walked off before they had a chance to answer. I don't know if they went to the bar together or not. They must've gone somewhere, because Andrea picked up a biker boyfriend the next day...

~~~~~~~~~~~~~~~~~

"Hi, Mark!" Dino said. This was the great thing about being young. Short memories. A few hours and all is forgotten. Not forgiven; just forgotten. "Meet Andrea's new boyfriend!"

Andrea was draped over this tall, thin guy with a lot of tattoos & a cigarette hanging below his mustache. "How do. I'm Brian." He held out a hairy hand for a shake.

"Hi, how's it goin'?" I asked, not really expecting a reply. It's one of those rhetorical questions. I learned about them in school. It's just like saying 'Hello, how are you, don't tell me, I can tell you're pretty ok, I mean, you're not dyin' or anything.'

"Brian's a biker guy." Andrea looked up at him with such love and devotion, so proud of her new boyfriend's occupation. "You should hear some of his stories."

Brian looks a little sheepish, which is weird for a hairy biker guy, unless maybe it's a black sheep, a tall one that likes to smoke. "Ah, it ain't nothin'."

Andrea hits him in the ribs. "Come on, that's not what you were telling me last night!" What is it about fat chicks? They like to hit skinny people. The mere mention of last night brings out the French in both of them. I thought maybe I should leave & give them a little privacy. I'm sure glad he's not kissing ME. Like sucking on a Brillo pad.

"Come on, you two," Dino interrupts with a smile. "Let's go get some drinks."

Now, you may be thinking that all we ever did was go to the Union and order drinks. That's not true. Sometimes we walked around, you know, took the scenic route to the Union. And sometimes we just stayed home and drank.

We had a fun time at the Union. Brian told us all about how he'd been riding with these guys for years, about his initiation into the gang, which by the way is so gross I'm not even going to describe it, but let's just say it involves blood and no it's not from an animal, and about how he's been in knife fights and stolen cars and had all these big adventures. He looks so cool sitting there leaning back with his cigarette dangling off one side of his dark face and ashes falling down onto his shiny leather jacket. Somehow the conversation turned to sex; don't ask me why, it just did. Maybe because Andrea and Brian kept hanging all over each other like teenage baboons in a breeding cage.

"You know what they say, once you've had black, you'll never go back." Andrea said this the same way she's said everything since she met Brian. She says it, turns, smiles, and they make out. "There just aren't any big white guys."

Dino turns to me. "I know."

WHAP!

My arm shot out all by itself and I landed a good blow right across her chest. I'm sure it didn't hurt. Not much anyway. Felt good to me, though.

"Uh, huh, huh..." Dino exaggerates pain.

Andrea laughs, "You deserve that!" And she did, too. Now the score isn't so uneven: Dino, about a thousand hits, Mark, one! I wear a devilish little smile.

"I guess I did." That's as close as I ever get to an apology from Dino.

"Hey, you guys want to go over to my apartment?" Andrea had a place on the north side; not much, but it was a mansion compared to the Roach Zoo.

"Sure!" Dino responded. "That'd be cool."

If Dino said it, that settled it. Which was OK by me, since I was such a wimp... I mean, such a caring, understanding guy.

"I have to meet some people, and I'll catch up with y'all in a little bit." Brian had such a cool voice. Sounded like his throat was bleeding.

"Great, I'll drive you," Andrea said. "You guys want to come with us?"

"No," said Dino the Decision Maker. "You go ahead. We'll get some more beer and take the bus."

And with that, we were off. We made it to the apartment OK. Dino hit me once because she saw some big-breasted blonde bounce down the stairs off the bus in front of me. OK, one thousand and one for Dino, but I still have one hit! We meet Andrea in the parking lot and she's not too happy.

"OK guys, who's got a knife? We got trouble."

"What trouble?" Dino asked.

Andrea looks panicked. "I don't know. Brian called and said he was coming over, but there's some other biker guys that are mad at him, and be prepared, he'll be here any minute."

"So, why are they mad at him?" I asked.

"I don't know. But there's some stuff going down and we got to be ready. Let's at least get some kitchen knives or something."

OK, I'm a little nervous now. Mrs. I-come-from-New-York-and-I've-seen-it-all-and-nothing-scares-me is worried her new biker friend is bringing a gang war into her apartment, and me & Dino get to be right in the middle of it. I've never been in a fight in my life. I wouldn't know HOW to use a knife. All I ever do with a knife is slice bread, and that's easy because it's not trying to slice me back.

We fill our pockets with ice picks, knives, sharp forks – anything we can find. We don't know what we're doing. Maybe Andrea does, but I sure as heck don't. I'd probably look really stupid pulling a bunch of silverware out of my pocket in front of a gang of fierce street warriors. Finally, Brian shows up. Alone.

"Honey, are you OK?" Andrea looks nervously past his shoulder. "Where are those guys?"

"What guys?" Brian doesn't look nervous at all.

"Those guys you told me about on the phone, the ones that were going to come over here and start a big fight?"

"Oh, they're just some old friends of mine. They were just kiddin' around."

"You mean it's no big deal? You big jerk!" SWAT! She hits his leather jacket. "We were scared to death some group of killers was going to come over & start a knife fight!"

"Really? I'm sorry baby," Brian said. He looks amused, like 'Oh, isn't she cute? She thought someone might kill her.' "Were you all worried like that?"

Andrea looks at us flatware carriers. "Yeah, everyone want to pull out a weapon?" We didn't answer, or pull out our very dangerous weapons. Those two just attached themselves to each other, arm in arm and hair in hair like a couple of magnetic rag dolls and we all walked inside.

You have to know something about Andrea and Biker Brian. Neither one of them are into celibacy. And the fact that we were there in the same room with them didn't seem to bother them at all. Me & Dino were lying on the floor, with a couple of chairs to block our view between us and the bed. We tried hard not to laugh at the sounds we heard. Every once in a while Brian would pop his head over the chairs and say something like "Wow, you guys are really getting it on now!" or "You sure are burning up the rug!" All we were doing was holding hands. Bad as we were, I think they had us beat in the don't-be-shy department. Later, Andrea is in the shower & Brian's sitting on the bed.

"You know, guys, I really love Andrea. I think I want to spend the rest of my life with her."

"Really?" I replied. I was kind of surprised. I figured he just got a chick in each town.

"Yeah, I tell ya. I've been all over this world, and I've done lots of things. I just want to settle down, you know? Start a family." He's pretty sober now, and he doesn't look scary at all. He looks tired.

"So, you thinking of asking Andrea?" I asked.

Brian sighed. "Yeah, ever since I met her, I just can't think of anything else. It's lonely out on the road. Yeah, I had friends, and girls, but you know, nothing is as important as family. I just want a family, maybe a few kids, a house. Being in a biker gang isn't all it's cracked up to be. I'm not so sure Andrea thinks the same way I do, though." Brian was right. Andrea liked him because he was a wild guy on a motorcycle.

"Wow. So you really don't want to be in the gang any more, huh?" I asked.

He looks at me with a little more seriousness than I'm used to from him. "No, I don't. I just want to settle down and start a family. You guys are lucky. Y'all'll probably get married & have kids & stuff. And you guys never had to do the kinds of stuff I did. Y'all are lucky." He sits there staring off into space for a bit.

Wow. That's all I can think of. What a shift of reality. He sure doesn't look like the marrying type. Don't think he'd fit into the elementary school PTA too well, either. But I guess he's telling the truth. He sure seems sincere.

A few days later, he popped the question. Actually, I think he more or less begged her. Us guys are like that – a tough act on the outside, but our guts are all soft & squishy. Andrea didn't want any part of it. I met them outside her apartment, at night.

"Come on, baby, won't you at least look at it?" Brian begged.

"No, I don't want it. I told you no." Andrea had her arms crossed & looked the other way.

Brian looks at me. "You want to see what I got her? It's a really cool stereo. It's not one of those old-fashioned kind, it's got a cassette, and a record player. It sounds really cool."

"Sure, I guess so." I didn't know what to say. I hate being the one somebody talks to when he's in a fight with his girlfriend.

"No, I don't want that thing in my apartment," Andrea piped up. "I told you I don't want to get married. I don't want any gifts from you."

Brian's still looking at me. "She won't even look at it. I worked hard to get that thing." He never mentioned paying for it. He turns back to Andrea. "I want you to have it because I love you."

Andrea shifts her weight uncomfortably. "I don't care. I don't want to marry you and that's that." Women can be so cold some times. But at least she's decisive. Nobody gonna put marriage chains on her.

Brian looks defeated & tired. "All right. I'll go. But you keep the stereo. I want you to have it." He puts on his helmet & roars off out of sight.

"Good!" Andrea says decidedly. Only when he's gone does she start to cry & lean on Dino's shoulder. I felt so sorry for that guy. I never saw Biker Brian again. I really hope he finds someone to start a family with. He'd probably make a really cool dad.

Chapter 11: Holy Pizza

"Why do I have to slice this thing into 10 slices? It's too hard," I complained.

"That's the way they want it. Ten slices each." Have you ever tried to slice a pizza into 10 slices? Eight slices is easy. You cut it in half, then half again, then half again & half again. Even 6 or 12 would be easy, but with ten you have to eye-ball it. "And you have to deliver them at exactly 9:30, all ten pizza's," my boss added.

The Catholic school wants these for their little rug rats. It's their Pizza Day. I chose to take this delivery, because I was Catholic. I was baptized, I was confirmed, I was an altar boy; so what if I'm living with my girlfriend, dropped out of college, drink, smoke, take drugs, hate my parents and play bass in a heavy metal band – I'm still Catholic, aren't I?

I arrive at the door precisely at 9:29 and 30 seconds. "That'll be $65.50 ma'am," I announce to the smiling little grey-haired lady at the door.

"OK here you go." It's a check. A check for $65.50. Exactly. "Bring the next batch at 10:30," she adds. OK I can do this, I think to myself. It's for God. I just delivered 100 painfully divided slices at exactly 9:30 and I didn't get a tip. I usually got a dollar or two per pizza, so I should have gone back to the shop with ten bucks in my pocket, but instead I get the warm cozy feeling of helping out a charitable God-type place. Wonderful.

I do this every Friday for awhile. It gets old, helping God out by giving him my tip money.

"That'll be $65.50 ma'am."

"Here you go. You think you could try to do a better job slicing the pizza's next time? Some of them were a little uneven."

Grrrrrrrrrrr

"Can I ask you a question? Why do you guys never tip?"

That took a little guts. Asking money from a Nun or whatever she was. Probably made God go "Humph! That's wasn't very nice!"

"Oh, OK, wait here just a minute. Gertrude! Oh, Gertrude, the pizza man wants a tip..."

They get a couple of the old ladies together & they scrape up the most amazing tip.

Two dollars.

Two dollars for cutting dozens of pizzas into 10 perfect slices, giving up tons of regular tip money, delivering them all on time, all for two dollars.

No problem. It's better than nothing. At least they KNOW they're supposed to tip now. Life will be better, and I'll still be a good Catholic.

The next Catholic rug rat pizza day, I'm smiling, I'm carrying ten freshly sliced deca-pie's (that's Latin for 10-sliced pizza's).

"That's $65.50, please."

"OK here you go."

A check. I stare at it. It's a check all right. For sixty-five dollars and fifty cents. I stand there for a second. She walks off, starts to distribute my beautiful carving work to a lunchroom full of children that are staring at the long-haired teenager that mysteriously appears with their food every Friday. I blink. I squint. It still says $65.50.

Well, OK, that's it. Being Catholic is too darn hard. I go back, we make some more pizza's, I slice 'em up into 8 sorta-even slices each. Oops, I showed up a little late. I get the darn check for $65.50. I tell my boss, get someone else to do this job, I won't do it any more. No problem, he says. Next Friday Jamal will do the school.

They never called & complained. I guess they could tell I was angry.

Up in Heaven, God's going "tsk, tsk tsk..."

Chapter 12:   Midnight Special

I'll give you the moral of the story first: Never complain about the food before you get it.

"OK, we've got a batch of specials ready for you!"

I was pumped. A gallon-and-a-half of soft drinks will do that to you. I had just returned from my last normal delivery in the sporty little truck. It was great. The company paid for these little Chevy S-10's, so you could drive them into the ground if you wanted to. I considered the delivery of a pizza an emergency. That made it OK to never, ever use the accelerator as anything except an on-off switch. Light about to turn green? Floor it. Light about to turn red? Floor it. Light already red? Slam on the brakes. Cop car next to you? Floor it, then let off at the speed limit, then get as close to the stop sign as you can, then slam on the brakes.

It's not without its detractors, unfortunately. One time when I was doing the slam-stop-floorit routine next to a cop, he ended up behind me, with those dreaded rolling lights in my rear-view mirror. I just loved being pulled over in front of the pizza parlor with my boss & co-workers staring out the window at me. At least he didn't make me walk a straight line.

"Excuse me, is there some emergency?"

"No. Just the pizza's." I felt a real camaraderie with other professional drivers. I'm sure he had to answer emergency calls too, every once in a while. "I saw you there, so I was very careful not to go over the speed limit." (In other words, I normally speed when you're not lookin'.)

"Has this vehicle ever been in an accident?"

"I'm sure it has! It's a pizza truck." I took great pride in that last sentence. Not only was it a pizza truck, it was truck #6. All the other trucks had huge, square propane ovens mounted on the back, with signs on them that said "Pantera's Pizza – Radio Dispatched!". The radios had long been removed from the trucks, and I'd never seen an oven used, but all the other trucks still had 'em. Truck #6 could really get up and go, without all that weight. And, of course, seeing as how you have to use some pretty inventive driving techniques to avoid traffic – running through alleys & across curbs & such – it's probably been in a few wrecks. Heck, maybe a few dozen.

"Why has it been in a wreck?" Like, OK man, I just told you, it's a pizza truck.

"It's a pizza truck." There, I said it again. Hurry up, man, pizza's are waitin'.

He looks over the truck for a good while, then calls something over the radio. Meanwhile, my boss & pizza buddies get bored & go back inside. Finally, he comes back over to talk to me.

"Well, I suppose you're right. It must have been in a wreck. When I called in the plates, it came back as a GMC, but looks like it was rebuilt with Chevrolet parts. I thought it might be stolen." A smart thief would definitely go for this truck, that's for sure. "Try to keep your speed down." And with that, he switched off his lights & went his way.

Fortunately, that didn't happen too often. Truck #6 was quite a beauty, but on this particular night I was in one of the slower oven-trucks, and believe it or not, the oven was lit up. It was the owner's idea of a promotion. See, we put this ad in the university paper: "Pantera's pizza – midnight madness sale – large pepperoni pizza for $5, midnight-2am." People were supposed to bring their cash up near the dorm, where one of us would be waiting. Give me a five, give you a pizza – it was easy.

Unfortunately, business wasn't booming. Here I was with about 10 large pepperoni pizza's, and maybe one or two people bought 'em. After 2 hours of being in that heated oven, it was more like 10 large cardboard circles with hard cheese on top. In fact, when I got back, my boss gave me a fresh one.

"You need to deliver this to the dorm, room 550. He said it wasn't fresh."

"Really?"

"Yeah. I couldn't blame the guy. He said, 'Just listen to this' & threw the pizza in the box. Sounded like a Frisbee!" An unhappy customer. Oh, well. It happens.

The next night was the last night of the "sale", and we didn't bother going down there. Figured nobody would show up. So we packed everything up, cleaned the kitchen, threw out the dough & mopped the floor. We were all hanging around talking, but my boss was on the phone. He didn't look happy. We had the juke box going pretty loud, so I didn't hear what he said. I saw him slam the phone down once & it just rang again. Finally, he puts it down & comes over to us.

"We're going to have to do the special tonight."

"What? No way! Who was that?"

"It's some guy from the college paper. He says we advertised it, so we have to do it."

"Tell him to forget it."

"I did. I even hung up on him, but he called back. Something about your rights & the law. I guess we'll have to make some more pizza's."

"You want us to make some more dough?" That was rather time-consuming. We made like 50 pounds of this stuff in a huge, I mean huge mixer, and throw the ball of dough into a trash can (one that we clean out, by the way) until it rises. It'll fill up a big trash can after a couple of hours. But I didn't think we had a couple of hours.

My boss looks beaten. "We'll have to pull it out of the trash. Go open the dumpster."

When we dump out the leftover dough for the day, we get a big black trash bag & throw it outside the kitchen, into the dumpster. We actually had quite a bit left over, and it was still there. Someone pulled it out & set it on the floor. I do have to say that at LEAST we pulled the dough out of the middle, after we ripped the bag open, and I don't remember any roaches crawling on it, even though we had quite a few that hung around waiting for an old pizza. And it was still fresh. Sorta.

I got to be the one to meet the angry mob at the dorm. Why didn't anybody show up yesterday, when we HAD pizza's? To tell the truth, they weren't too bad. A little irritated, and I got the impression they had all been standing there talking about us. They kind of had a little smirk of victory on their faces, like they'd just won a fight with a woman (I've never actually had that experience myself). I think we even gave them a big discount, like $1 each. I'm sure there were only a couple of them who actually WANTED a pizza; they probably just stopped everyone that passed by & told them, "Hey, we just called this pizza place & got mad at 'em, & they're bringing a whole bunch of pizza's over here for a dollar each! Yeah, we threatened to make up a bad story about them in the paper..."

They got their pizza's & left, and I sat there waiting for more customers. I sat, & sat & sat. Finally, it was 2am and I had a ton of leftovers. I called my boss on the phone in the lobby.

"I've got a bunch left over, you just want me to sell 'em to the cops or somethin'?"

"Sure, just sell 'em real cheap. Get rid of 'em."

So I waved down a campus cop & made him a deal.

"Would you like to buy some pizza? We've got a bunch left over & we're just going to throw them away."

"How much?"

"How about 25 cents each?" He seemed surprised. Didn't know cops got surprised.

He gets a couple of bucks out & buys the whole load. He tells his buddies on the cop radio, "Hey, everyone, we've just gotten a bunch of food from Pantera's pizza. Meet me at the station." Just then some jerk races through an intersection (crazy driver – why do people do that?). The cop says, "Thanks! I guess we won't be pulling any Pantera's Pizza trucks over any time soon!" and zooms off. Yeah, I bet you won't. Maybe you'll change you mind when you chip a tooth on a petrified pepperoni fossil.

Back at the shop, my boss is in a suddenly wonderful mood. "We have some time now, and I'm going to show you how to close the right way." Full of energy, smiling. Usually, when we close, we sweep, throw out the dough, take out the trash, finish the dishes – the normal stuff. Man, was he motivated! We wiped, we cleaned, we scrubbed. He even had us armor-all the trash can wheels. I have to admit, though, they did look good. The whole job took a couple of hours, but hey, we've got the slickest casters in town now!

I found out later he'd gone by his apartment & snorted some cocaine while I was gone. "There! That's how a store SHOULD close!" His voice had a triumphant tone to it, and he wore a silly smile as he looked around the kitchen, beaming with pride & glassy eyes. I wondered if he'd remember any of this.

It was 4am by the time I went home that night. The bed – uh, the mattress – felt wonderful! I must've slept for 10 hours. This working for a living sure takes a lot out of you.

Chapter 13:   Worst Thing I Ever Did

"I'm late."

Now, usually, my response would be, 'We'd better get going!' but I had since learned another meaning to that phrase. It wasn't good news.

"How late?"

"A few weeks." OK, this is bad.

She was "late" when I met her. Turned out to be nothing, which is good because the father could have been either of those jerks that raped her the prior week or two. That was a relief. (You know, come to think of it, my prior girlfriend from high school had been raped a few years before I met her. What is it about me? Traumatized women find me attractive.) But despite the consequences, which we viewed as dire, we had gotten more and more careless, even after a scare last month.

We got a pregnancy test at the store, and confirmed the bad news.

"What are we going to do?" I was lost. I didn't want a baby. She didn't want a baby. My parents know we're living together. Her parents do, too. Both sets of parents hate it. We're not married. We have so many fights, and I mean some real knock-down dragouts, I can't see us raising a child. Probably turn out to be a little Hitler or Manson or Boy George <shudder!>.

"This is going to kill my mom," Dino said. "This'll put her over the edge." That's true. Her mom was right on that edge, and kind of teetering back & forth. Dino's mom was really nice to me, but she was suffering from depression. Dino's sister got killed in a car accident a few years earlier by a drunk driver. No one in that family was normal after that. Rusty, her brother, routinely went on a drinking-and-driving binge & ended up in jail. Her dad had spent thousands on, let's say, "contributions" to keep him out of prison. I guess that can explain some of Dino's personality, such as her hatred of religion. She was devastated after her sister died; totally devastated. I don't think you can really appreciate that until it happens to you, but having dated a mentally disturbed woman for two years, I think I can say that it really messes you up. She came to school the next day, or a few days later, after the accident. Some bright cheerful girl saw her & said "Hi, I heard about your sister. Too bad. But don't worry, she's in Heaven now!" with a huge smile. What an idiot. I don't blame Dino. She might have been right, maybe she IS in Heaven, but for gosh sakes, show a little compassion! I'd've wanted to slap her.

Anyway, we talked about our alternatives.

"We could give it up for adoption," I ventured.

"No way. If my mom finds out I'm pregnant, I'm afraid she'll kill herself. She can't find out."

"Well, what else can we do?"

"We can get an abortion." Holy cow. An abortion. Sure, I've put my faith through some real ringers lately, but killing an unborn child? That's definitely on God's do-not-do-this-or-else list, isn't it?

On the other hand, lots of people do it. It's totally legal. And on top of that, most people don't think it's really a human until it's born. Just a fetus. A medical procedure. No biggie.

"I don't know, Dino."

"We have to. It's the only way. I don't want to do it either, but we don't have a choice."

"Maybe we could wait awhile. Maybe you'll start soon," I said with a tinge of hope.

NOT!

We waited a couple more weeks, and of course nothing changed. I spent some time calling some places. I looked in the phone book under abortion. Terminating pregnancy is a big business! There's almost as many ads under abortion as there are lawyers. I called a couple of places that looked like they do it all the time.

"Hello?"

"Yes, do you perform abortions?"

"Yes we do. We have a doctor on-staff that performs the operation on Tuesdays and Thursdays. Has your wife had a pregnancy test yet?" Wife? She's not my wife! Let's deal with one catastrophe at a time here.

"Well, we got one at the grocery store, and it came back positive."

"Well, we really need to get her in here for a test to make sure she's pregnant first."

"I'm pretty sure she is. She's about 8 weeks late now. Can you tell me how the abortion is performed?" I brace myself to get really grossed out.

"Yes, certainly. First of all, we can't perform the abortion until she's missed her period for 10 weeks. That's so the fetus is large enough that we can see it to make sure it's been removed." The fetus. Right. It's a fetus, just a thing growing in Dino's tummy. Just a thing. "Then we use a suction device, inserted into the womb to remove the fetus. It's painless and she can go back to work or home the same day. Takes about an hour."

"OK, thanks." I also asked about the cost, which turned out to be about $200. Kind of a lot for me at the time, but I wasn't worried about money. The rent could wait; this was a much bigger problem.

I called a couple of places that didn't answer me so directly.

"Do you do abortions?"

"We have a group of people here who would like to talk to you about your choices. Let me schedule an appointment for you."

"But you don't do abortions, right?"

"We would like to talk to you about how to solve your problem. We have a lot of very good video's on different things you can do."

"Uh, OK, thanks anyway." <click> The last thing I need is a video from some Christian outfit showing me how awful abortions are and how people want to adopt babies so bad. I believed Dino when she said her mom couldn't take it.

I also did some research at the library. I pulled a half-dozen medical books down & read about the size of the fetus at 10 weeks, the different abortion procedures and how they're done. I saw a picture of a 10-week old fetus. It had a big head, and little bitty fingers. Darn. I wish it didn't have the fingers. Looks almost human.

"I read up on it at the library," I told Dino. "Even had pictures. Looks like no big deal."

"Did you see any pictures of the baby? Does it have little toes & fingers? I don't want to do it if it has toes & fingers." She didn't like the idea any more than I did.

"No," I lied. "Not really. It doesn't even look human." Maybe that's not a lie. Maybe that's a stretch, because it didn't look TOTALLY human. No hair, no lips, no eyelids. It looked like a fetus – an ungrown human being.

A few days later, we took a bus to the abortion clinic. I waited in the lobby for what seemed like a couple of hours, and Dino came out.

"OK, that'll be $200 please." I gave the smiling receptionist some cash (checking account? what's that?) & we walked outside.

"How do you feel?"

"I'm OK. Let's go." Dino hid her emotions pretty well. She hardly ever got upset. Mad, yes, but not upset.

"You want a cab or something? They said you shouldn't be walking for a couple of hours."

"No, I'm fine. Let's walk." There's no arguing with Dino. It's her way or the highway. She seems to be holding up OK. There're no little drops of blood behind us.

So we're walking from downtown over to the university district, where our apartment is. After a while I asked, "What was it like?"

"Oh, not too bad. The doctor could see I was a little upset about it. He kept telling me it's OK. There were a few of those girls from the massage parlor there, and they were laughing and joking about stuff. I think they go there all the time, instead of using birth control. I just think that's sick." Me too. "I can't believe people would just not care & say, 'Oh, well. If I get pregnant I'll just get an abortion.'"

"That's terrible." It was. After the stress of making this decision & finding out about all the procedures & seeing pictures, I couldn't imagine doing it so carelessly, like it's no big deal. But maybe it really was; what did I know. Maybe after the first one you can do it without being emotional.

A few days later, it was almost forgotten. But that's not the end of the story. No, sir. I wish it was. The truth is, over the following 10 or 15 years, I was haunted by what's best described as a "ghost of a child" that never was. I've had nightmares, where there'd be a plant growing, everybody admiring its beauty, and I'd say, 'Don't you people understand? Don't you know what that's going to be when it grows up?' so I uprooted it, hurled it over the fence & it turned into a little girl, that ran around & crawled up on my lap & just looked up at me. Or another one where I felt guilty about running over a small child, but I kept saying 'It's OK. I didn't break any laws.' The child never has a name. It's spooky. I never know what the dream means until after I wake up, and then I realize it's about the abortion, and I get a cold chill like I just realized I saw a ghost.

Even though I wasn't the doctor performing the abortion, and even though I wasn't the one who was carrying the baby – uh, fetus – I feel terrible guilt because I was so instrumental in finding a clinic & researching it. I even told Dino I thought we should do it. I think it was at this point in my life that I decided not to even try to be good any more. How could God forgive me now, after all I've done, and especially after doing murder? That's on his top ten sins list. After that, I really didn't care anymore.

Chapter 14:   The Band That Never Was

To think that I ever had enough talent to be a professional musician is quite amusing to me now.   There's just something about being young and energetic that makes you think you can do anything.   Maybe the hormones were clouding my vision, or maybe I was still hanging onto that idealistic 'I'm special' mentality.   I'm going to be famous.   Won't everyone be surprised when they see me on the TV news, smashing my bass into a police car!   I'm going to be the best musician ever...

NOT!

Before college, my best friend Crash and I would get together and 'jam'.   I have to say, his mom was one of the most patient people I have ever met.   When you're first starting out playing, you have to play loud so you can hear yourself.   Never mind that you sound terrible, and outside dogs are barking and car alarms are going off; you think it sounds great, because there you are, total stud muffin wearing a guitar, slung down to your knees, even lower than your hair, with skin-tight jeans and a black concert jersey.   Boy, we were cool.   Boy, we stunk!   And all through this, Crash's mom would smile & sometimes get us drinks & snacks.

One particular jam session at my house, we were trying to put music to a beautiful verse I had composed while in school.   I entitled it, 'Screw the Establishment.'   It went something like this:

Arise in the morning already adorning

The dreary day ahead with powder shots of lead

Now change seats you have seven minutes to go

Don't be late or it's punishment you know

Hi hello excuse me hey you there

You know you're all alone, get your act together

Don't drink don't smoke don't snort don't toke

We are the elders, do what we say!

"OK, that sounds good.   But we need to do that part a little faster."   Crash was talking about that final climactic line, 'We are the elders, do what we say!'   At the moment, I was on the microphone & he had his guitar, and we'd patched both into my stereo system to make a recording.

"OK, we'll do it fast now."   We ran through the song again until that last line

.... "We are the elders, DOWHATWESAY!"

"Sheesh, Mark, that's too fast!" Crash was laughing in a kind of annoyed way. "Let's try it again."

"OK." I wasn't supposed to be the singer anyway. Good thing. I stunk.

... "We are the elders, do WHATWESAY!" For a bass player, I had an appalling lack of rhythm.

"No, Mark, like this. 'Do – what – we – say'." Crash repeated it so I wouldn't miss it. "'Do – what – we – say, Do – what – we – say".

I joined in. "Do what we say, do what we say, do what we say!" Hey, I got it! "Yeah, do what we say, we are the elders! Yeah!" Crash hit that last chord with extra gusto. "Then there's a guitar solo..." I said as Crash wailed away with his tremolo bar. Done deal – good song.

We never did perform 'Screw the Establishment' for anybody. Actually, the only person we ever performed for was Dino and her friend Dorothy, there in the university dorm. But we were too shy to play one of our own songs, so we did some really simple cover tune by Judas Priest or something. We were each playing through our boom boxes (no amps – you kidding? amps cost money!) and at the end, we cranked them both up full blast (which on a boom box ain't that loud, but it made a funny noise) and rubbed the strings of Crash's guitar and my bass together. It sounded really unearthly. Our audience was suitably impressed.

"Oh, that was great, Mark! Cool!" Dino was convinced I was on my way to stardom.

"Cool. Thanks." Crash was wearing a coy smile behind his hair barricade, but I could tell he liked it too. The girls were smiling big as they gleamed up at us from the dormitory bed. To them, we looked almost as big as we did in our own eyes.

While it's nice to have an audience, and the girls were really impressed by our theatrics, in the end Dino & Co. split us apart. Crash accused her of being in college for an 'M.R.S. degree.' I was blind to it, just plain ignorant and stupid. (Kind of like I am now, but with more hair.)

"No way, Crash, I can't believe you think that!" It was painfully obvious.

"Maybe so, but it sure seems to me, like she just latched on to you..." With both hooked claws, and bared vampire teeth. Of course, he was right. But I was blinded by lust – I mean, love.

"Don't say that, Crash. Dino really cares about me." Sure she did. You can tell by how many bruises I had on my arm.

"OK, what ever you say, man," Crash replied. He was such a cool guy. Never wanted a fight, even if I deserved it. I treated him like dirt, and only once or twice did he say anything about it. I wasn't going to listen to him no matter what he said. I was happy being entrapped – I mean, being attached to a girlfriend, er, I mean, having a deep, meaningful relationship with a fine, upstanding, moralistic southern woman. At least, I thought I was.

So, after spending every waking moment with Dino, and never sleeping, our little band kind of fell apart. He got his own girlfriend. He just went to the mall and picked one up. There's all these 14 & 15-year-old girls that live there, and they just wait around & when a cool-looking guy walks buy, they stick on him like a gummy worm on a movie theater screen. Every time I saw Crash after that, his accessory was glued to his right side, and Crash wore this see-what-I-got smirk on his face.

He dropped out of college too, about the same time I did. Both of us managed to squander thousands of dollars of our dads' money, but I just wasted it on tuition. Crash was smarter. He took it to the music store and got himself a real amp, and just told his parents he was in college. Instead of living in the dorm, though, he lived at a Co-op. It's where a bunch of people share the expenses (and work) of a big house in the middle of town. It was pretty cool. I went there to eat one time, and some guy – it was his turn to cook – made ravioli. I had never seen 6-inch pasta-wrapped beef before. The only ravioli I had ever had was Chef Boyardee.

"I have only one question. What is it?" It was a joke. I was used to complaining about the food, like in the Dorm's Bolemia Maker's Cafe, but I hadn't quite gotten the concept of the cook being someone I know or who had feelings.

Nobody laughed.

I just held my peace and sat down with my Giant Ravioli. I felt better when no one else popped it in their mouth, but cut it up with a fork & knife. Don't know how I'd get that huge thing down in one bite.

It's neat the way they decide on new members. They have a meeting. Everybody's there in the living room, where people, you know, live, and this guy (or girl) gives the head honcho lady an application. Then he (or she) goes into a back room & waits while everyone talks about him (her) behind her back. On one of my more energetic fights with Dino, I was depressed enough to sign on at the co-op. I was sure we'd never get over THIS fight, it was so bad. (We did.)

They were all looking over my application. "Oh, I see you're a musician," said a tall blond girl with a clove cigarette in her mouth. Her hair looked like it was frozen in a moment of time, that instant when you get out of the shower & shake your head like a dog to get rid of all the water.

"Yeah." Interesting hair. I wonder how she made it do that? I tried not to stare. "I'm not in a band yet, but I play bass."

"You know, you can't practice late around here," said a chubby guy with glasses. Poor guy couldn't afford real ones; he had to use Coke bottles. Or so it seemed. "No one makes noise after 10:00." He seemed very serious. And tired.

"I know. I don't make much noise." That was true. Sort of. "I'm just another starving, hopeful musician trying to make it big." The city was full of people like me. I'd met so many people that were going to 'make it big' that I started thinking, maybe I wouldn't. After my last fight with Dino, I didn't think I had the strength to, anyway.

"OK, well, we'll let you know in a minute," said the head honcho lady. She ushered me in to a back room, where I couldn't hear a thing. Darn insulation.

About 20 minutes later, I was brought out. "OK, you're in. Welcome to the Co-op." That was good news. Housing around there was ridiculously expensive. And apparently I wasn't offensive to anyone there. Just one person has to disapprove, and I get denied. Guess the Giant Ravioli cook wasn't there that day.

"Great. I guess I'll let you know in a few days. A lot depends on my girlfriend."

There was an understanding look in HeadHonchoLady's eyes as she nodded her head. "OK, well, we hope you'll stay with us." Turns out I never lived there. Me & Dino made up – sortof – and Crash and I never really played much again.

There was this other guy that didn't make it into the Co-op. I felt sorry for him. I just happen to be around when they had this meeting. The poor guy was in that back room for probably an hour.

"I don't know if I want a gay guy here," one person said. "I might catch AIDS."

"He seems nice enough," another offered. "But I don't know..."

"Well, I don't want him bringing any of his boyfriends around here," some guy said. The thought kind of nauseated me, too.

"Well, we've seen YOU here with YOUR girlfriend before," another one countered. "Isn't that the same thing?"

No, of course not. Gross.

"Look, guys." HeadHonchoLady was getting impatient. "We can't turn away someone just because he's different." That's true. Just in this room, I can see seven different colors of hair. "We need the money."

"But what good is the money if we all get AIDS and die?" That guy has a point. "He's going to be using the same toilet as we are, isn't he?"

"I don't think we can get AIDS like that," a girl said. Actually, nobody knew. This was the 1980's. We thought if a gay guy farted we were all gonna die.

After a long time of this bickering, the gay guy came out of the closet (so to speak). "Uh, we're not done yet," LeaderLady said.

The guy looked anxious and impatient as he peered out around the open door. Looks almost too normal, with his plain brown hair & thick plastic glasses. "I don't mean to be pushy, but I've got somewhere to go. I just need to know, one way or the other." Poor bushy-headed gay guy; he'd been in there for an hour.

"But we're still talking..." LeaderLady said nicely. I guess that's a nice way to say, we're still deciding if you're too disgusting for us to take your money.

"Look, I've been to four other co-ops today, I just need to know now so I can try another one." He had a little anger in his voice, but not much. I think he just wanted out of the closet.

"Well, we can't all agree on it yet." I'm glad LeaderLady was talking, because most of us didn't want to say anything in front of the guy.

"Fine." The bushy-headed gay guy picked up his backback & walked out the door. Everyone was quiet until LeaderLady broke the silence by slamming her books down.

"I don't see how we're going to pay the bills if we turn away everyone who wants to live here!" She picks up her books & storms out.

Everything is quiet again. People eventually walk off back to their rooms. Like I said, I feel sorry for the guy. He's just like us; just has a thing or two backwards.

But the end of my relationship with Crash was not the end of my music career. (And NO it wasn't that kind of relationship! Stop thinking that way!) At the pizza place, I had met Larry. Now, Larry was a REAL musician. He was skinny, wore black leather, had long hair, and liked to play fast riffs on his Stratocaster. Crash was more of a hammer-them-chords/ear-bleeding-distortion kind of player, in a mellow, yeah-I'm-cool kind of way. Like shooting a machine gun from a lazy boy recliner.

"So, you play bass? I didn't know that. Cool." Larry was a fellow delivery guy. He could race through the alleys with the best of 'em. "I've been wanting to start a band. We should get together & jam some time."

"Sure! That sounds like fun!" I said enthusiastically. Larry was a nice guy. He had that Van Halen hair thing going on, lots of energy. We made up some songs that would make you dizzy they changed chords so fast. We had one in 5/4 time, which drove me nuts trying to play it. ONE-two-three-four-five-ONE-two-three-four-five.

But, alas, it was just me & him. Back to just a guitar, and just a bass. No drummer. Until one day.

"Hey, Mark, I met this guy the other night. He plays the drums and he wants to come over and practice."

"Cool." That sounded good. I was a little nervous, never having played with a drummer, but looked forward to doing more than sitting on the couch talking about how famous I was going to be or throwing notes out to try and keep up with Larry's chord changes. "When is he comin' over?"

"He said tonight. He's a nice guy. I think you'll like him. Sounds real serious about starting up a band. He used to be this major alcoholic, but he says he's going to stop."

"Alcoholic?"

"Yeah," Larry shrugged it off like it was no more serious than a pimple. "He like beat up his girlfriend & ended up in jail or somethin', but all he wants to do now is play music." What is it about drummers, anyway? Bang, bang, bang.

"Cool." That sounded fine to me. What the heck. We can't be too picky. At least he wasn't gay. Drummers are hard to come by; probably because they're all in jail.

The drummer guy was OK. He talked a lot. He played OK, from what I little I knew about rhythm instruments. He could bang those drums real hard and loud, and it sounded really cool. We ended up practicing at this guy's house, friend of Larry's. He had a real big living room, with stairs and a loft. I was there playing bass while Dino & Mr. BangBang's girlfriend watched. (Larry's girlfriend wasn't there; I saw a picture of her once. I think she lived with her mom – not old enough for college or anything; looked a lot like Crash's girlfriend. Must've been shopping at the same mall). They watched & listened while us three tried our best at the 2112 Overture by Rush. I thought it turned out pretty good. The girls liked it, too.

Everything was going OK until Larry's friend came home. He was a bass player, too, and a friendly one because over the next 30 minutes or so the room was filled with teenagers all up the stairs & on the loft. They all came over to watch the 'jam session'.

I was petrified. OK, playing in front of one or two strangers was one thing, but this was a bit much. I felt like one of those doctors doing a heart transplant in a glass operating room, while experts from around the world peer down from their seats & critique my work. So, instead of playing like I usually do, throwing notes out as fast as I can, I settled into a Jimi Hendrix repeating rhythm while Larry & BangBang ripped the room apart. I was having fun, I guess, until Larry's friend wanted to borrow my bass.

"Sure." No problem. Go ahead and borrow my baby; I don't care.

So this guy proceeds to take my bass, and pump out some of the coolest riffs I've ever heard. Him & BangBang went at it for 30 minutes, boom-chic-a-boom-bada-boomboom-chicachica-boom, slapping & popping those strings so hard I thought they'd fly across the room. It sounded really cool, and everyone was getting into it. After it was over, he said, "Mark, you want a turn?"

Me? Solo with a drummer? In front of all these people?

"Nah, thanks." I tried to sound cool about it.

"You sure?" He couldn't believe I didn't want to 'jam'.

"Come on, Mark, why don't you play?" was Dino's response. I tried to act like, hey, I could do that too, but I just don't want too. "No, thanks. I'm fine." He handed me back my baby. It was good to have it back in my hands.

I felt awful. Some stud-muffin musician I turned out to be. Some jerk friend of Larry's can out-do me just by banging a few notes out with the drummer. He made it sound so GOOD. I don't know. I guess I just didn't have the rhythm in me. Not like I didn't want to. I swore I'd get better. Next time, it'd be me with the drummer, and in front of a lot more people than this!

So, we planned a practice. Oh, wait, not this day; I have to work. This day's not good; BangBang has to go visit his kid. How about Saturday? BangBang's busy. Why not just you & me, Larry? We could work on a few things. Sure.

Later, we're walking over to Larry's place, me & Dino. Larry meets us on his scooter.

It was a nice winter day. Me & Dino were drinking Slurpie's from 7-11. "So, we gonna jam today?" It felt good drinking something cold in the cold weather. Don't ask me why.

"Nah, I've got something else to do."

"What's that?" I ask.

Larry sniffs. That's his secret way of saying, cocaine.

"So, you going to go get some?" Larry was spending more & more time looking for, buying & doing cocaine lately, and less & less time on the band.

"Yeah, I think I need an ounce or two."

"OK, well, have fun!" Dino said.

"You two have a good time. We'll work on our songs later..." As Larry puttered off to buy more drugs, me & Dino walked around a bit. I was glad the practice was called off, because I didn't want to work on anything. I'd gone to my job already, I had a Slurpie in my hand, a girl at my side, the night was clear & crisp. I just wanted to walk around, talk, make out. (This was one of those times me & Dino WEREN'T fighting.)

I got to thinking about things. Me & Crash weren't going anywhere with the band. Larry & BangBang didn't have any time to practice. I didn't even have time to practice on my own. Dino hated it when I practiced anyway. This town was filled with musicians who practice for hours every day. I'm never going to make it. I can't even play in front of a couple dozen teenagers at someone's house; how am I ever going to get on a stage in front of a few HUNDRED strangers? How am I ever going to be anything more than a teenager on the streets of Austin, walking around in the middle of the night freezing my butt off with my fat girlfriend?

And so began the slow realization that my dream was dying. I was a nobody, a failure. I didn't even get a chance to really try, and I was already beat. I would never be important, special, or even unique. I was just like a thousand other people in this town. A lousy musician with no hope of success, no future and no band.

I was nothing.

Chapter 15: Girl Gone-Gone

Things with Dino got gradually worse and worse. I would get more and more stressed as we fought more and more often. For some reason, I couldn't handle the idea of a breakup. I was attached to Dino; I'm a very loyal person, even to a witch. It was going to take a lot to cause me to break up with Her Hauntedness. In the end, it was her that left me.

One of the hardest bones we chewed on was how to make a living. I wasn't in college any more, and my parents didn't send me any money. Dino's parents didn't either, of course – we were on our own. So, I worked. She stayed home. Sounded like a good relationship for a family with kids and a white-collar dad, but I was a pizza guy and Dino had no reason to not work. On top of that, we abandoned our Roach Kingdom for a beautiful, I mean absolutely stunning apartment a little farther north. Expensive, in other words. I don't think I ever saw a roach in that place, and it had real carpet in it. And Dino did work for awhile, but she had quit that job and didn't feel like getting another one.

I spent many months delivering pizza, until I saw this big sign up at Dobie Mall: telephone solicitors, now hiring, $6/hour. That was a TON of money! I might even be able to pay rent with that with one paycheck! I had done soliciting before in Houston. It was a hellish job. We called farmers and asked them page after page of questions about their crops and what insecticides they use. Most of the farmers were very, very patient, if a little hard of hearing.

"So, how many acres of soybeans did you grow this year?"

"What?"

"How many ACRES of SOYBEANS did you grow THIS YEAR?"

"Soybeans?"

"YES, SOYBEANS. HOW MANY ACRES OF SOYBEANS DID YOU GROW THIS YEAR?"

"Oh, let me see. I suppose about 15. Fifteen acres."

"And which of the following products did you use on your soybean crop:"

"Huh?"

"I said, WHICH OF THE FOLLOWING PRODUCTS DID YOU USE ON YOUR SOYBEAN CROP:"

"Soybeans?"

"YES, SOYBEANS! WHAT DID YOU USE ON THEM? WHAT KIND OF PESTICIDES DID YOU USE?"

"Oh, well, I use that Lasso. It works good. I've been using it for years."

"And how would you rate the effectiveness of Lasso on your crops last year. Poor, fair, good, very good or excellent?"

"What?"

This would go on sometimes for 30 minutes. I'd have to take a break after something like that. Of course, a job like that, you don't get breaks except when everyone else does. Then we'd stand around the bank building & smoke & drink Cokes, which I stole out of the Coke machine by stretching my fingertips inside it. If you reach waaaay up, you can feel them in the racks. Just flip them over a little, just a little bit, and PLOP you'd get a free Coke! I was always nervous a banker working late was going to catch me, but that made it more fun. Nowadays, they have a bar there so you can't reach in.

I felt so sorry for those farmers. This was in the late 1980's, and nobody made any money. I remember asking a guy what is gross expenses were. $500,000. And what his gross income was. $500,000. What was his profit for 1985? Zero. I don't know how they managed to pay their bills. At least they had lots of food to eat. I bet a lot of those farmers are out of business today. Maybe they all got jobs as phone solicitors.

So when I saw this sign, I thought, yeah, I can do that. I've done that before. Sure. Wow. Six bucks an hour. Not only that, I only had to work a few hours a day. They'd only call people & harass them at night, from maybe 6-10pm. Heck, I could make the same money in 4 hours that took me 8 hours at the pizza joint.

OK. This is how it works. You have your pre-filtered call list. A list of prospective customers in the immediate area, sorted alphabetically by last name. The list we had were all supposed to be TV Guide subscribers. Better than what we used in Houston during the non-farmer surveys we did. They made us use the phone book. You use a ruler, and you go down the line & call these people cold-turkey. It went something like this.

"Hello, can I speak to Mr. Slow?"

"This is Mr. Sleaux." I botched everyone's name mercilessly. There're some pretty weird names out there, for sure.

"Hello, I'm Mark with Customer Research." Sounds official, doesn't it? "I'm calling to check and make sure your subscription to TV Guide is working OK." That's a lie. I should have said, this is Mark, wanna buy more magazines?

"Uh, yeah, it is. I think so."

"It's showing up on time, no problems?"

"Yeah, sure."

"OK, good. Let me write that down here." I scribble in the air with an imaginary pen. "While I've got you on the line I'd like to tell you about a special offer we have on renewals, just for our special customers like you. We'd like to extend your TV Guide subscription and give you four more magazines for five years for only $5.99 a month. That's five years of any magazine we offer, plus your TV guide that you already get, for five whole years for only $5.99 a month. Now, which magazines would you like?" Another lie. We just gloss over the fact that they get one year of TV Guide, but five years on the other magazines. And 99.99% of the time, they'd hang up on me, usually after saying something rude. No kidding. I'd make 500 calls a night, and score maybe 3 subscriptions. By the end of the day, I hated everybody.

It gave me a headache like you wouldn't believe. I used to get awful, awful migraines in those days. The boss was real helpful one time when I didn't have any aspirin. I asked him if he had any.

"Yeah, sure, here you go. How many you need?"

"Oh, give me a bunch, I've got a real big one."

"OK, here you go." He poured out about 20 pills. No problem. I usually took at least twice the normal dosage. I can't even feel the normal one.

I swigged it down with Coke. Now, I've heard that if you mix a LOT of aspirin with Coke, it'll make your stomach bleed, but I didn't believe it until I started to feel light-headed. Maybe it was just the headache playing tricks on me, but it's the same feeling I get after I give blood. Kind of woozy. I'm surprised I didn't kill myself overdosing on pain killers, I did it so much.

So after a night like this, you can imagine how happy I was to go home and find Dino asleep on the couch amidst a pile of Ding-Dong wrappers. Ding-Dongs that we couldn't afford, by the way.

She did finally got a job. Just think, you've got someone you care about, you're working every darn day supporting her and yourself, you want to keep her safe, and she goes out and gets a job downtown where she has to work late hours in a rock-n-roll record store selling records, incense, drug paraphernalia to all the freaks & weirdo's. OK, so maybe I was one of them, but I didn't like it. Remember, she'd been raped twice when I met her. It's not like she's got some Goddesslike immunity to harm.

"I'm going to be working late again."

"How late?" I was getting annoyed. She wasn't getting off until 2am lately.

"Oh, about 2 or so."

"You want me to come walk you home?" That's something I usually did. I hated the idea of her alone on the streets downtown at that hour.

"Nah, I'll just take the bus. I'll be fine."

"The last bus leaves at 2, doesn't it?"

"Yeah, I think so. I have to go."

Dino was a good worker when she wanted to be. She'd put in 10, 12, 14 hours at a time. I don't know how she did it. Maybe she has an energy bank built into her. Sleep all day for three months, work like crazy for one month. Of course, she made me feel guilty as heck 'making her' work. Now she can say I'M the lazy one, because I was only working a few hours every day. Sure, it's a little bit each day – it's called regular income. Duh.

I took the bus down there anyway, even though she didn't really want me to. I wanted to make sure she was OK.

"Hi, Dino."

"Oh, Hi." She puts down a magazine.

Did I mention they sell pornography there? They have a room in the back, and men would come in, hand her a dollar 'browsing fee' & disappear behind the wall. Well, guess what magazine she's reading.

"What are you reading?"

"Oh, I was just looking through this. It's really just stupid."

"What do you mean? You hit me if a girl walks down the sidewalk a mile away, and you're here reading Penthouse?" I was angry. Doesn't sound fair, does it?

"Oh, Mark, come on, it's no big deal. I don't even like it. I was just so bored, being here all alone." She knew how to pull my chain. My fault she's here. My fault she's having to work so hard. My fault she's alone with a sex-crazed maniac browsing the rags in the back.

Just then I saw a car stop on the street, and this old lady (old means late 20's or better) comes in & starts grabbing records off the shelf by the handful.

"Can I help you?" Dino asks.

"Oh, I'm just fine, thank you." She's wearing a smile, but she doesn't seem happy. "Donny owes me some records."

Donny was the owner. A big fat guy that showed up every once in a while and had questionable morals. When Dino signed on, Donny said "We don't always listen to the government when it comes to taxes. That bother you?" So the fact that he used records to pay some lady was not out of the question. I thought it was weird. I thought she was stealing stuff.

Mrs. SpeedShopper was gathering quite a load. When she couldn't fit any more into her arms, she headed for the door. I moved in front of the door to block her way.

"Get out of the way, you silly idiot," she said with a bit of a British accent. I looked at Dino.

"Just let her go. I'll call Donny."

So I stepped aside & let her go. She threw the records in the car & sped off. Dino called Donny.

"Yeah, there was some lady in here, said she knew you. She just picked up a bunch of records; said you owed her or something." There's a long pause. I can just make out the sound of someone yelling on the other end of the phone. "Well, what did you want me to do, stop her? Oh yeah?" She pulls the receiver away from her ear. "Right, I'm fired," she said incredulously, and with a SLAM hung up the phone.

"What was that all about?"

"Donny said that was his girlfriend. He's coming down here. He's pretty mad." Dino was pretty mad, too. Didn't look scared at all.

Me? Afraid that a large lawless man who just got ripped off by his ex-girlfriend is going to come take a few records worth of hide out of my girlfriend? Of course not.

Yeah, that's it. 'NOT!' is right. I was NOT scared; let's just say, worried.

I was ready to take him on when he walked in the door. I wasn't going to let a little fear get in the way of protecting my girlfriend. Sure, she did something stupid; I would've fired her too. But this guy might want to even things up his own way.

Donny walked in and I assumed my best fighting stance. Since I've never fought anyone, I don't know exactly what that is, but I was giving him the cold evil hate-you kill-you eye, and that should be enough to show him I meant business. He glanced at me and lumbered over to the cash register. "You two just get the hell out of here."

Dino slings her purse around her shoulder & walks to the door. "You can fire me if you want to, but I will sue you if you try to hold my check." He looks up for a second, pauses & then goes back to counting his cash.

"I'm not going to hold your damn check. Just get out of here and don't come back."

And that was the last we saw of him. We found out later he'd asked one of Dino's co-workers, "Does her family have any money?"

"I think her dad is rather well-off," was the answer he got. So he never pursued it, knowing Dino only had to call a lawyer or the IRS to totally ruin him.

We rode home on the bus together, and didn't say much. That was how her 'jobs' went. I worked a boring routine, day in & day out, same job, same pay, and she gets this terrible job, it's a roller-coaster of working late, dangerous walks home, strange clientele, and poof! no more job from Dino and I'm still grinding away at the Pizza joint, or harassing people on the phone. To this day I never hang up on a phone solicitor. They have just about the awfulest job there is.

I got so desperate I even asked her to marry me. I know, I know – stupid stupid stupid. Fortunately, she declined. She wasn't as dumb as I was. She said, ask me again in a few months. She knew there's no way it'd work out, the way things were right then. I was trying to give her the one thing I remember she always wanted. I was hoping it would make a difference.

It didn't.

I got so tense once I tried to kill myself. I was depressed. I didn't think I could live without Dino, and she had left me alone when I was all sad & everything and I said to myself, life is not worth living without her. I'll just take a couple of puffs every few minutes until she comes back, and if she doesn't come back, I'll just be dead.

I had asthma. I remember when I was a teen-ager I had asked my doctor what would happen if I took too much of my medicine, which came in a little 'puffer'. "If you consumed the entire contents of this puffer, you would probably die," was his matter-of-fact reply. I was hoping for something like, "8 or 10 puffs will cause hallucinations & disorientation; a few more will lead to euphoria and a sense of non-reality." He just said, overdose and you'll die. If he had told me that several times the maximum dosage will make the heart stop cold, I might have taken him more seriously. Deep down, I didn't want to die anyway; just get a little attention. I really believed I would just get sick & pass out or something; I had no idea how fatal that stuff really was.

I took a couple of deep, long puffs, held it in as long as I could. Damn, I'm depressed. Dino hates me. She's going to leave me. She doesn't care about me. Another couple of puffs. It's been five minutes. Doesn't she know how upset I am? Doesn't she care that I'm going to die? Nobody cares. Two more big, long puffs. I don't care either. I'll just die. I'll just kill myself because nobody cares. No one will notice if I'm gone anyway. To heck with Dino. To heck with me. I go for a couple of more puffs...

That's strange. I could've sworn this puffer was full a second ago. I shake it up & try again. Empty. How weird.

I'm not going to say that it was a miracle, but I will say I don't know how that puffer got emptied out like that. I was very fortunate, to say the least. There are several reasons why I deserved every bit of that inhalant, but Someone Somewhere had different plans for me. Maybe Someone Somewhere can somehow use a pathetic old hippie to do some good in this old world. Maybe. Or maybe it's just dumb luck.

Dino eventually came back, and I told her what I did, and even though we were in the middle of a big fight she said if I'd called her, she would've come back to save my life. She once told me, you may find someone else to love you, but I don't think you'll ever find someone to love you as much as I do. Maybe she did love me, but not as an equal. She loved me like a pet, or a young child, or even a baby. And that wasn't good for me. I felt abused, controlled, totally de-masculinated and worthless.

Dino finally left me. I couldn't leave her. She called her mom (a real nice person; she liked me a lot), they packed her stuff up & drove off. I was left alone in the apartment for the first time in over a year. I went inside, lay on the bed & tried to cry, but nothing came out. I guess I wasn't really that surprised. I didn't want to be alone. I went and got my friend Crash & we went for a walk together.

"I want a Playboy." That's a magazine, for those of you lucky enough not to be exposed to trash like that. We walked all over the place, and I got the guts up to go into an 'Adult Reading Room.' It was nothing more that a store with magazines on the shelves, all with naked women on the front and enormous boobs that don't even look human, and dark rooms in the back where men silently watch movies.

"Can I help you find somethin'?" I turn around to face the guy behind the counter.

"I'm just looking for the basics, you know, Playboy, Penthouse," I said, trying to look cool but knowing I wasn't doing a very good job at it.

"Oh, we don't carry that stuff here."

"OK." Fine. Good. Go away. Must leave. The only thing worse than being seen in a place like that is being seen by someone you know, and I knew that guy behind the counter. I had sold him my stereo about a month earlier. I made a hasty exit, and pretended I didn't hear him say "Hey, hey. Hey!" I think he recognized me. Whew! I made it outside.

So we went to Stop N Go; a nice, safe place to buy some candy, a coke, and oh yeah can I have that magazine there in the black wrapper? I was free at last. I could look at anyone I wanted to, and Dino couldn't hit me or get mad at me any more. No one was going to hit me ever again.

I took out the big picture in the middle & plastered it on the wall. There. See, Dino, I'm looking at someone else. Why don't you come hit me? What? Because you're not there? You ran away with your mommy back to Dallas?

It didn't work. I still felt lousy. I hated my job. The band was non-existent. I couldn't go back to college, even if I wanted to. Dino was gone. There was nothing for me there in Austin any more.

It was time to go home.

Part II

Chapter 16:   A New Father

Godfather, that is. A new Godfather. But not the kind that smokes cigars and gives you an offer you can't refuse, unless it's on a pizza. Godfather's pizza was a nice little strip-center place with tables, chairs, a kitchen, and an opening for an aspiring young delivery boy.

Bobby was the manager there. He had 5 kids that he never saw, because he was always at Godfather's. He's the one who hired me.

"So, you've delivered pizza before?"

"Sure, I have." I was a pro in my own eyes. I also now had a car, albeit a used family sedan with 100,000 miles on it, but it ran good. "I delivered pizza in Austin for almost a year."

That impressed him. Imagine how thrilled he was to just by chance get a professional pizza man applying for a job at his restaurant.

He looks back at my application. "So, why did you leave Austin? It says here you were in college."

"Well, it didn't work out too good." I didn't really want to dig up the past. I just wanted a source of income. I didn't really need it; I was back living at home, with my parents. Dino was gone. She was my past. She's a done deal, a closed book, a finished story. I needed to move forward. "I tried to play music, but that didn't work out either." I was getting mad at myself for saying more than I wanted to. "But I know the area real good cuz I grew up here," I added for good measure.

His eyebrows raise up, and I can tell I've just about won him over. When he said "We pay $4.50 an hour, plus tips for delivery," I knew I had him.

"Sure, that sounds fine. When can I start?"

"Right away. How about in the morning?"

"Great!" I was excited. New city – well, old city, but you know, a change anyway – new job, new (first) car. Bobby shows me around the kitchen, I say high to the bread-roller, and the guy putting toppings on, and the guy smoking a cigarette in the break room. Everybody said hi back, except the guy with a cigarette. I don't think he spoke English.

The job at the pizza place was just a side thing for me. That car that I was driving – the family sedan my dad gave me – it wasn't just an old beat-up car, really. My dad had wanted to fix it up first, so us three – me, Dad & my brother – pulled the engine & rebuilt it. We pulled it all apart, took the block down to the car wash & hosed it off, and put it back together with new rings, bearings & gaskets. A few months and 3000 little bitty parts later, tada! new car!

I enjoyed working on cars. I liked driving cars. I liked going fast. I even liked the family sedan, because it skidded a lot. Sure, it took a long time to get up to 70mph, and it felt like the fenders were dragging the ground when you turned, but I drove it like it was a hotrod.

Me & Crash used to go driving together. Besides Michael-Scott, I can attribute Crash with influencing my driving ability. We used to take our cars – our dad's cars, I mean – to the local elementary school and go round 'n' round the parking lot, until I was afraid my tires would pop. We'd be coming back from the 7-11 and I'd say "left!" and Crash would turn hard. "Right!" and he'd skid around again. One of Crash's favorite sports was driving home from school. We were all nerds. We didn't do football, or basketball, or any other real sport. But I think Crash had the all-time best altitude record in the subcompact-hatchback category. There was this long road in the subdivision, past a bunch of houses, with a stop sign at the end, but right before it, the road took a little dip. He'd floor the little Toyota and get up to 60 or 70, hit that bump, sparks flying, lock the wheels up, and skid to a stop right at the stop sign. We had to quit after he messed up once, though. Some kid was playing in the front yard, and Crash overshot a little, and we kinda skidded to a halt about 3 feet from Daddy's little baby, and Daddy looked like he might want to kill us, so we kinda didn't go home that way any more.

I developed a rich love of cars that way. I wanted to fix mine up & make it go faster. It would have been nice to start with something that had a little more potential, but I wasn't discouraged. Where there's a will, there's a way, right? Well, I was spending a lot of my money at the auto parts store, getting new shocks, plugs, wires, little stuff like that. I said to my self, self, yes, you, I'm talking to you, self, uh, I forgot – oh, yeah, uh, self, you enjoy working on cars, why not become a mechanic? Sounded like a natural idea to me. Go to school, get more money when you get out. Mechanics make good money, don't they?

Well, I enrolled at the local junior college. The entry requirements for the auto school were a lot less than at UT. Basically, you just have to have non-counterfeit money, and they let you in. I learned a lot there. We took our cars apart, and did something exciting like balance the tires or change the brakes, then put them back together again. It was fun.

I practice my driving techniques at my new pizza job. After being tutored by Crash, then the traveling abroad to the Austin School of Evasive Pizza Delivery, I was one good pizza man. I once delivered 27 pizza's in one night. Sure, the lady who ordered that last one was asleep on the couch, the husband was angry at having to wait 2 hours for dinner, and he made me call my boss & we gave him the cold pizza for free, but hey, you shouldn't order pizza during a football game. He had it coming – we were way too busy.

The pizza place was where I met someone special. Peter. Let me tell you about Peter.

Peter was younger than me. Peter was a little unstable. Peter was very emotional. Peter had never really worked anywhere before. Peter's parents were broke up. Peter was a little unstable. Peter liked weird music. Peter liked me. Peter was a little unstable.

We seemed to relate to each other pretty well, and after work I gave him a ride home. He didn't have a car at the time. He said, let's go listen to music in a dark parking lot. OK. Sure. I don't have plans. I wasn't doing anything else at 2am anyway.

We pull into the school parking lot and Peter starts playing this weird punk stuff, where these guys are all expressive & full of feelings. Groups like The The, Depeshe Mode. I don't remember all the weird band names, but it's like the exact opposite of Judas Priest screaming out LIVING AFTER MIDNIGHT! The singer was going on about how he feels bad and nobody understands him and he needs to be loved. Peter is splayed out on my hood, acting out the singer's anguish, staring into the sky with a cigarette in one hand and making flailing motions with the other one. His lips are mouthing the lyrics.

"What do you think he means?" asks my contorting new acquaintance.

This was typical of the deep, philosophical discussions we would have. "I think he's having a hard time fitting in or something." I gave it another moment of intense thought. "Maybe he just broke up with his girlfriend."

Peter thinks this over a bit, rolls off my hood, takes a drag of his cigarette & says "I think it's because he's gay." His eyes are locked on mine. He is very intense. This is apparently a big deal to him, I think to myself. I find out later, though, that everything is a big deal to Peter.

The song changes and he starts to mouth the new words like he's singing TO me. "Who can understand, what makes a man, it takes another man, to understand." And with that, he twirls around with his arms outstretched, as if carrying this huge, invisible emotion ball that suddenly crushes him as he lies motionless on my car, again.

"Peter, are you ok?" I was trying to act calm. This guy might be weird, but he's not dangerous. What's he going to do? Spin me to death?

He gets up & faces me with that intense gaze of his. "I think my girlfriend might me pregnant." He said everything with such gravity. Oh, my God. End of the world! Stop everything! We have an emergency here! Peter's girlfriend might be pregnant! Life cannot go on!

After the stunned silence wore off, I said, "Really? What are you going to do?"

Peter looks away, takes another pull of smoke in. He never answered anything right away. Had to experience it, live it, feel it, BE the question. He finally responds with, "I don't know. I don't know what to do."

Well, being the older, wiser one present, with so much worldly experience, I responded with, "Have you thought about an abortion?" Why not? After all, I'd just gone through this with my own girlfriend. What's the big deal?

He pondered that for a bit. "I don't know. I think Kellie just doesn't want to face it." Everything he said ended with an unspoken "know what I mean." Kellie was his girlfriend, by the way.

"Well, my girlfriend just had one. It's easy. You just go to the doctor; doesn't take long at all." OK, so I hadn't gotten to the old-enough-to-feel-guilty-for-teenage-mistakes-such-as-murder stage of my life yet. That would come later. And thank God he didn't take my advice.

We stayed there a couple of hours, listening to music, me standing there enjoying the peaceful night air, Peter on my hood writhing in emotional anguish. As the evening becomes dawn, I drive him home & dump my weary body in bed, trying not to wake my parents. I'd never been around anyone like Peter before. I felt a little sorry for the guy, and almost fatherly. I mean, heck, I was 19 or 20 at the time, and he wasn't even out of high school yet!

Chapter 17: The Brain Club

"Uh, Mark?" It was my mother's voice. Her head was poking into my doorway above my headboard. I was not in the mood to wake up after finally getting to sleep.

"Huh?" I said in my usual I'm-dead-leave-me-alone style.

"Mark, there's two people at the front door. They say they know you." Mom seemed real curious about this. She'd never seen any of my friends at the door before, except for Crash, and certainly not so early in the morning.

"What time is it?" I sat up, trying to think, who do I know in Clear Lake anyway? I just moved back to town. Who could it be?

"It's about 6:30". Wow. I'd been asleep for what – two hours?

So, I stumble out of bed & amble down the hall to the front door. I open it, and there's my new friend Peter, staring at me, while a girl – Kellie, no doubt – standing next to him. She's not looking at me. She's looking at the ground. I quickly surmise that at least SHE doesn't think it's normal to wake up a friend two hours after keeping him up all night, especially a friend you just met a couple of days before. He doesn't know me that well.

"Oh, hi," was all I could get out.

Peter said, "We need to talk." He was serious. This was a big deal to him. Obviously, he had gone to his girlfriend's house, talked to her about something important, and brought her to me so I could talk to her. How weird that sounds. I hardly know HIM and he's bringing his girlfriend over to meet me?

Speaking of his girlfriend, as I showed them the way to my bedroom, you know, she doesn't look bad at all. She had long hair, with wispy bangs across her eyes, thin, shapely. She tossed me a smile that said, sorry about this, and say, she's pretty! I liked her face; she seemed, I don't know, approachable. I thought, I don't want to show Peter pictures of my old girlfriend. His is much prettier. Meanwhile, my mom is staring at this group of people with quiet amazement. I can tell she's just bursting to ask what's going on, but she just stands there holding her hands.

Peter takes residence up in my brother's bed (he's in college) and Kellie sits down on the floor. I sit on my own bed, hugging a pillow and trying to blink the sleep out of my eyes. Now I can get a good look at her. What a pretty mouth. She has such a warm smile, and beautiful hair. I didn't give much thought to my own appearance; typical guy, I guess. I still had the hair down to my waist, I hadn't shaved in a couple days, no shirt, smelled to high heaven. Didn't seem to bother my companions a bit, though.

"This is Kellie," Peter said matter-of-factly. "Kellie, this is the guy I told you about, Mark. He's SO smart."

Kellie looks up at me & smiles another embarrassed smile. "Hi. I'm Kellie." What a sweet voice. And I just love that mouth. I think I want to kiss it ...

Hold on, I'm not getting into that again. I was very happy to get rid of a witch of my own, thank you very much; I don't need to fill my life up with pain and misery again. Besides, she's taken. She's Peter's girlfriend.

Peter looks at me. "She's pregnant." His words carried the gravity of a death sentence. "She doesn't want to have an abortion."

"Really, why not?" I ask.

Kellie shrugs. "I don't know. I don't think I could do that to a little baby." She looks at Peter. "Besides, maybe I'm not really pregnant."

"I know you are. I just feel it," Peter replied. "You just have to face it." Kellie didn't answer. Peter looks at me as if to say, can you talk to her? I can't get through.

Gladly.

"So, if you really are pregnant, what do you plan to do? Give the baby up for adoption?" I couldn't imagine actually keeping a baby. At that point in my life, getting pregnant was an illness to be avoided at all cost.

"I don't know." She looks down. "I guess I could keep it." I can tell she feels on the spot, like us guys are grilling her alive. She doesn't get mad, though. Interesting.

We talk for an hour or two, about all kinds of deep philosophical stuff – not just pregnancy. Things like emotions, feelings, you make me feel like this, well, I feel like that, doesn't this mean this. Finally, with the sun midway up the sky, we part ways. Peter takes off on his bicycle, and Kellie starts walking home.

"Wait a minute," I call out to her. "Let me give you a ride."

She just smiles back. "No, thanks. I can just walk home. It's not too far."

"It's all the way in Meadowgreen, right?"

"Yeah, but I walk around all the time. It's no big deal."

"Are you sure? I don't mind. I like driving." OK, so I had ulterior motives. I wanted to get her in my car. I wanted to see what she was like when not being dominated by Mr. Freakazoid.

"Well," she hesitated. "OK. Sure." So, I opened the car door of my little white economy car, and after shoving the mound of old Zinger wrappers and chocolate milk cartons into the back, I officered her a seat.

Peter was gone down the block on his bicycle by this time. It never occurred to him that bringing his girlfriend over & leaving her with me might not be the best idea he ever had.

"So," I started. "You like walking a lot?"

"Yeah. I walk all over the place. I like to walk down to the 7-11 and get Slurpies."

"Me, too." I was finding a connection here. This was good. "Me & my friend used to walk around all night. It's real nice, except the cops kept stopping us 'cuz they thought we were doing something bad." Bet that impressed her. I was old enough to get harassed by the cops. "Besides, I hate the daytime. I just can't be cheerful when the sun is shining."

"Me, too," she replied. "I just hate it when my mom wakes me up in the morning, all bright and cheerful. I like it better at night."

"Yeah," I agreed. "I mean, how can you function that early in the morning? Sometimes I sleep until it's almost dark outside. It's great." Actually, sleeping until midnight was sounding very good to me by them.

We chatted a little more, and she directed me to her parent's house. She said bye, thanks for the ride. There were some kids playing in the front yard. One little girl squeaked "Kellie!" and ran into her arms. I was amazed. I'd never met a girl that was good with children before. Very impressive.

I drove off, thinking about what had happened over the last 24 hours. I met an emotionally unstable weirdo. I met his attractive, totally sane girlfriend. I drove her home, and she seems to like me OK, and her crazy boyfriend trusts me for absolutely no reason. Pretty neat. Maybe....

Aw, heck. I'm tired. Too much thinking makes you nuts.

I got back home and my mom greets me at the door with "Well???"

"Well, what?"

"Well, who were they? They were very interesting." She'd been waiting at the door for me to come back. Most exciting thing in her life since the winter Olympics on TV.

"Just a couple of people I met," I answered non-chalantly.

"Boy, they sure looked serious about something." Mom was enthralled.

"Yeah, they're both real smart." Then, thinking back on our deep, intellectual conversations, I added, "We call it the brain club." My mom's eyes are big and round with interest. I turn and head to my room. "'Night."

Bed. Must reach bed....

Zzzzzzzzzz.......

Chapter 18:   Pizza Joint Buzz

There were some interesting people at Godfather's pizza. You've already met Peter, the emotionally unstable flame-in-a-gas-tank ball of emotion. He was a good friend, if you don't count the fact that he was immature and looked to me as a parent or guide. We spent a lot of time together, talking about things & driving around.

One night, I was driving through the college campus with Dr. Emotion, and we stopped to talk in the car awhile. I used to enjoy that campus, late at night, with the cool air blowing in my open window, watching the mist from the building air conditioners blow past the parking lot lights. Very relaxing, and yet, giving me a sense of mechanical power and eerie electric force. Unfortunately, the campus cops didn't like hippies hanging around in their turf. Usually, they ran me off, but this time, they caught me with a minor beyond curfew hour.

"Excuse me, sir, can I see some identification?" The officer was standing back a piece for safety. I smiled at the thought that he was actually scared of a wimp like me.

"I can assure you, I'm quite harmless," I advised as I got out & fished for my driver's license.

He takes my license, hands it back, then shines his flashlight at my companion. "What about yours, son?"

Peter was visibly scared. He'd never been accosted by the police before. "He doesn't have a license. He's only 17," I offered.

The man frowns. "I'll have to call his mom. You're not supposed to be out this late unless you're 18." Peter gives him his mom's phone number, and nervously waits.

"What's going to happen?" he asks.

"Well, we're just going to call and make sure your mom knows you're out here, and she's OK with it. If she doesn't press charges, you'll be free to go."

I made small chit-chat with the plump policeman while we waited. I wasn't scared at all. This was one of the nicest cops I met on my evening escapades. Most of them treat me like a crook. He answers a radio call, and informs us Peter's mom is on her way.

"She's coming up here?" Peter asks.

"Yes, she'll be here in a few minutes." Weird. I guess most moms would take a call from a cop seriously, but if it were me, I'd tell the cop to throw my little delinquent in jail, and I'll see about picking him up in the morning. But I'm not someone's mom, so I don't know.

His mom shows up, thanks the officer, and then climbs into the car with us. She's a nice lady, a psychologist by profession, and just sits in on our conversation for a couple of hours, then leaves. We talk about rules, being young, what we're doing out here, but she never acts accusing or angry or even sleepy. Very cool.

My interest in cars was peaked when Brian started working at Godfather's. Brian was great. Brian was into hot-rods. Brian had a Camaro at his house, and every paycheck would buy another piece to make it go faster. It was up on blocks with a blown engine, but he had all sorts of parts in his house: cam, pistons, oil pump, heads. I really admired him. He told me lots about his adventures with his friends. His buddy had another Camaro, with a 400-horsepower or more engine. They'd drive it on weekends, street-racing & running from the cops. I don't think he ever lost a race with that monster. It had tires bigger than most trucks do. Unfortunately, I never got to see Brian's car completed, but wouldn't be surprised if he got thrown in jail for going 150mph in a school zone with it. Brian was so cool.

I would continually pick Brian's brain. What's the best brand of engine? What size valves are best? What kind of heads make the most power? What brand of ignition do you use? I was almost embarrassed to show him my hand-me-down special, but he was very encouraging about it. "Yeah, that's a cool car. It's light, so you could make it go real fast. What size engine you got in there?"

"It's a 225, slant-6," I said apologetically. "It's got a 3-speed tranny," I added. Three-on-the-tree we used to call it; as opposed to four-on-the-floor, which real cars had. I didn't tell him that I once clocked it going 0-60mph at 18 seconds. Almost as fast as a fully loaded bus with burned valves and three flat tires.

"Well, I think you'd probably want to start with maybe rebuilding it, maybe a new carburetor."

"Me and my dad just went through the whole thing; it's got new rings, and we had the heads done at a machine shop." I love being able to talk cars. Most people these days don't even know what a crankshaft is. They just want to turn the key & make it go when they push the gas.

Brian's sizing up my pathetic dweeb-mobile. "That's cool. Yeah. OK. You know what you really ought to do? You need to put a V-8 in this thing. Yeah, that'd be real cool. Get a 340 or something." Nice advice. Impractical. I remember the endless hours of work just to put the engine back in the way it was before. I wasn't about to yank it out again and try to make a different engine fit in there instead. What I needed was a new car. Something with some potential.

Enter: Craig. Craig was a good-ole country boy that delivered pizza in his old truck. He heard me talking to Brian one day and said, "I have a '68 camaro for sale."

"Really?" Wow. Camaro's are fast. At least, I think they are.

"Yeah, I've been meaning to sell it. There's something wrong with the engine, but it runs. I used to have a real fast engine in it, but someone stole it."

"Someone stole your engine?" And not the whole car? I was thinking.

"Yeah, it was at this restaurant. I parked, went inside & ate. When I came out, the hood was up & the engine & transmission were gone."

"How'd that happen?" I asked, fascinated.

"Some guy in a tow-truck was watching me. When he saw me pull in, he waited for me to go inside, then he popped my hood, strapped the engine to his tow truck & drove off. Ripped it right out of there." Craig didn't seem as angry about it as I probably would've been. "I have locks on the hood-pins now," he added.

"So," I ventured, "How much do you want for it?"

Craig blows out some smoke & answers, "I guess $1200." Lots of my friends used to smoke those days. So did I. Nasty habit.

I arranged to pay him his money; part in a stereo I sold him, then part now, then parts out of every paycheck. Everything verbal, no contract, just spoken trust. Naive, huh? Not even a handshake.

I was so excited. "Dad, can you help me pick up a car?"

"You bought another car?" Dad was surprised and wore a cross expression as he peered at me over his bifocals. "What about the Plymouth I just rebuilt for you?" Interpretation: you ungrateful little brat, you mean I just spent all summer fixing up a car for you and you're going to go buy a new one?

"But this is a Camaro," I explained. That should make everything clear; obvious, really. You just can't compare a Camaro to a Plymouth. One is good; the other is bad. One is embarrassing to drive; the other is awe-inspiring. Never mind that I'd only seen the car once, and knew nothing about its value, only that it was blue and had fat tires on it. It was the only car for me in the whole world.

My dad agreed to help me pick it up. I expected to get in & go roaring off down the street, but when I got there, it wouldn't start. My dad helped me jump start it, but it wouldn't turn over. Then we noticed that the left rear tire was flat. I found the spare in the trunk, but it was out of air. We drove to a gas station and filled it up, but it wouldn't fit right where the huge rear wheel had been. I fiddled with it for awhile, and got it on there, but I still couldn't start it. We ended up towing it home & parking it on the street.

And there it was. If you only looked on the side without the big dent, it was beautiful. It had slick lines. It had thick blue paint that had only chipped off in a few places. And the rear tires were so big the fenders had been cut to make room for 'em. You know, I believe cars have spirits. They really do. They are so much a part of their owner. I'd never have a problem with self-confidence in this car! This was going to be my companion; my friend. That's what 'Camaro' means, you know. "Friend." Yeah. "Friends don't let friends drive slow."

Well, as enamored as I was, the sad fact was it didn't run, despite its killer look in the driveway. Made my Plymouth look like a white box on four bicycle wheels. Never mind the paint job stunk, the floor boards were rusted out and the inside smelled like mildew. It had potential!

So began my first of many experiences trying to make a fast car out of garbage. Well, second, but the Plymouth doesn't count. I never really tried to do anything to that car, except tune it up. I decided to use my Camaro as a project car at auto school. I pulled the engine out, which was supposed to be a 350, but turned out to be a 283. Grrrrrr. Then I bought an old 350 Brian had, that turned out to be a 305. Grrrrrr. So I decided to just build up the 283. What the heck – it was a strong engine. With the right parts I could make it go really, really fast.

With the right parts. Which required money. Money I didn't have. Not that kind of money, any way. Money for things like, big heads to let more air in. Money I wish I had when I tried to resurface the heads in auto shop, and ended up ruining them so I bought a used set the teacher had. Powerpack heads, they're called, which is misleading because they're really not built for power at all. So, I ended up, after over a year of back-breaking labor, with a basically underpowered Camaro that didn't run right. It was embarrassing, because people would pull up next to me, and want to race, and take off, then slow down & look at me like, well? Aren't you going to floor it? The sad fact was, I had floored it. It just didn't do much when I did.

Anyway, I kept the Plymouth for my night job at the pizza place. I just kept telling it, see, you're getting all worn out and you smell like pepperoni, but look what you're going to turn into. That's right. A Camaro. So when I hammer you too hard in a turn or steer you over a curb or turn your tires into liquid rubber delivering a pizza, just remember – it's for a good cause!

There were some interesting people there at Godfather's, all right. But I was puzzled at why they just went home at the end of the day. I mean, in Austin, we'd stay there for hours, drinking beer & playing pool. Don't know if it was my attitude or the fact that I just sort of STAYED there after the place was closed, but they eventually got the hint. We started this routine of cleaning up, closing the doors, turning most of the lights out, then partying. The assistant manager (Bobby the boss wouldn't have gone for it) would open the beer keg, and I found out Peter was very adept at breaking video games. He'd jam a knife into the coin slot or something; you'd hear a couple of bangs & cracks, and presto! we had all the quarters we could want! Then in the morning, they'd call the vending company and complain about how "those teenagers" broke the game again.

We played Super Mario Brothers and Galaga until dawn sometimes. I made the mistake of challenging Brian to a Galaga duel once. I had heard him talk big about his car, his friend's car, his buddy's Camaro. It looked like fun, bragging. I wanted to try it. Besides, I couldn't possibly lose. I was a Galaga pro. So, I decided to try this macho-ego voice on for size. "Hey, Brian, how about a game of Galaga?"

"Yeah, sure, but I haven't played much." BWOHAHAHA! Just what I wanted to hear! "You think you can beat me?"

"Man," I started, with a bit more sway in my step towards the machine, "I could beat you blindfolded with 3 broken fingers!"

Brian smiled big. "So, he wants to be bad," he chuckled. "Well, let's see whatcha got."

I went first, took my video game fighter's stance before the console, and worked that joystick so fast it was blurry, while my other hand shot the guns like I was having a finger conniption fit. When I finally died amidst the onslaught of several hundred descending aliens, I proudly relinquished the controls to my adversary. Brian smiled, "120,000 points; not bad" and started shooting. Hey, he's not bad. Actually, he's doing quite well. Uh, oh – whoa. Thought he was toast that time for sure. Look out! Hey, how'd he get out of that one? Well, about 15 minutes and 600,000 points later, it was my turn to further embarrass myself. I managed a few more kills, but Brian whooped up on me pretty well, topping out over a million points. So much for being "bad."

During those nights we found a way to pipe our own music tapes into the PA system so we could listen to decent music. Peter brought his touchy-feely weirdo music, and twirled around in an emotional seizure for all of us to see. It started to get on everyone's nerves. He said some deep, emotional thing – not directly, but eluding to it, like the song is saying "I'm alive, and dead" and he'd say, "There's only one way..." and go rebounding down the hall like a gutter ball. They'd wait for him to get out of earshot, and say, Mark, you're going to have to do it. You're the only one he'll listen to. That guy needs a kick in the butt. The song would change, and Princess would come back, flail against the counter, say something else, smile, and go sit & stare at the ceiling with his cigarette dangling out of his mouth.

"A steel toe. A big, steel-toed boot just right in the ..."

We weren't the only ones having a hard time dealing with Peter's ego-centric psycho-trips. He apparently didn't score any points when he decided to dump his girlfriend. Kellie showed up one day (I saw her from the kitchen), and they exchanged a few words. Peter came back from the counter, & said "She wants to talk to you." He had a low, angry voice like something had just happened that made him mad and embarrassed him a little. I found out later that Kellie had brought him a self-addressed, stamped envelope and said with a smile, "Here's an envelope. Since you won't give me the money you owe me, you can put it in the mail. Is Mark here?"

Peter started to get on my nerves. You can expect, maybe during tough trials and really rough circumstances, someone may be distressed and need to talk about things, but not every day. Peter started to feel really comfortable around me, and acted like a disobedient child. He wanted to drive over here. He wanted to listen to this song. He wanted to go get ice cream over here. I felt more and more like a father figure, and like he needed some discipline. He rode with me on a delivery once, and while I was talking with the customer & getting the money, he was in my car, honking the horn & flashing the lights. Then he locked the doors and wouldn't let me in.

By this time, Peter had foregone the traditional dress of a modern teenage male, in preference for the delinquent-transvestite look. He wore makeup, spiked his hair up, and had a huge black trench coat that matched his high-top boots perfectly. If you didn't know him, you might actually get scared seeing him in your neighborhood. I finally told him off, something like "Look, you're going to have to behave yourself if you're going to ride with me."

"OK, fine! If you don't want me here I'll just leave!"

"Go ahead!" I didn't care. I was tired of being used and abused by this immature freak of nature. Sympathy and pity can only take you so far. So he gets out, slams the door and I race off.

Later, we were talking and I discover that not only has he been experimenting with cross-dressing, but is interested in cross-dating, too. He looks over at me, and says with grave seriousness, "Kate's not the only one I like."

<shiver!> Now THAT'S scary!

Chapter 19:   Kate and the Big Brown Monster

Kate was a girl at the pizza joint. Nice girl. Kinda short, with long hair, always wearing fluffy sweaters. I kind of fancied her a little, kinda cute, but so did Peter. I didn't do anything about it; Peter did, I found out. After I left the pizza joint, they were actually living together, until one night Kate woke up and saw Peter standing over her with a knife. He said, oh, I wasn't doing anything; I was just looking at the knife. Kate got spooked, and called his mom, who called the local mental hospital. They came & picked him up & took him to the funny farm for a little while, and that's the last time I saw him. So much for Peter. (I hear he got out a little later, having successfully manipulated the caretakers into believing he was sane, and went to live downtown in the Montrose area, which is renowned for gays, crime & drugs; I'm sure he fit right in.)

Well, while some people might just gun-ho goforit when they see something they want, I'm not that way. I like to just wait it out, go slow, get to know someone, and if it works, it works. OK, so I've never done it that way before, but there's always a first time. Anyway, me & Kate were just friends, and I was still feeling burned by my ex, so we just spent some time talking together, no big deal. I didn't want a relationship, no sir, not me.

I mentioned to Kate once that my parents had never gotten me a dog before, boohoo, and I'd always wanted one. True story. I really, really wanted one, so bad that one time I made a Christmas list several pages long with just the words "a dog, a dog, a dog" over & over & over again. My parents never got me one. They said they were worried with my asthma that I'd have a reaction to the dog hair & end up with an iron lung for the rest of my life. Small price to pay for the undying love of a little puppy licking your cheek, but who knows; maybe they made a good decision. I did get my mom once to ask the pediatrician if a dog would upset my asthma. He said it'd be fine as long as it wasn't a long-haired breed. They still didn't get me one. I think the real reason is, they didn't like dogs. My dad had a dog when he was a kid. It used to follow him around & he'd feed it and every few days it'd disappear for awhile & come back all beat up & tired. Then one day it disappeared into the woods and never came back. Maybe my dad didn't want me to have to deal with the loss if it ever ran away; who knows.

Kate's parents had a kennel, and Kate had told me about this one dog named Condor. He was a Belgium Shepherd, big, strong dog, purebred, but they had to keep him on a chain because he fought with the other dogs. He'd climbed over a 6-foot fence once, and ripped up his underside good. I was impressed. My kind of dog. Fearless. Strong. Untamed. Cool.

Well, it was my birthday, and Kate had made me a chocolate cake & brought it up to Godfather's on her day off. I was so touched it made me cry. <sniff> Nobody had ever made me a cake before, except for my mommy. <sniff> Thanks, Kate. Thanks a lot!

"I have another surprise for you." She had a deceptive little grin. "Look in the back of my car."

I warily peeked in the rear of her hatchback, and this giant, black nose appeared in the glass. It was a dog! A BIG dog.

"It's a dog," I concluded.

"Yeah, it's Condor, the dog I told you about." She came up to my side. "Mom can't keep him at the kennel any more, so you can have him if you want him."

I was beyond description, overwhelmed, touched and totally floored. This girl I don't even know very well has given me the one thing that has been missing from my childhood, the one boyhood desire that had never gotten fulfilled (except for that dream with the cheerleaders and ... uh, never mind).

"Kate, thanks!" I hugged her & didn't say anything for a while.

"So, you like it?"

"Yeah, I love it!"

"Here, why don't you say hi?"

She opened the hatchback, and Condor came out, wagging his big tail and panting a friendly hello. His big teeth glistened in the streetlight as globs of slobber dripped down from his immense jaw. I took hold of the inadequate little leash & he hopped obediently to the ground.

Kate was watching me. "He likes you," she observed. "He usually doesn't take to strangers like that."

I was kneeling beside my new pet beast, giving him a big hug. "Aw, he's just a big baby. Aren't you a big baby, Condor?" Condor licked my face & sniffed me all over. I was in heaven!

"Thanks, Kate! He's perfect!"

"You don't have to keep him if you don't want to. We'll take him back if your parents don't let you keep him."

Parents. Ha! I didn't listen to my parents. Besides, they'll certainly see how happy this dog makes me, and let me keep it, no problem. Never mind that it's not my home, it's theirs, and they probably don't want a hairy dinosaur living in the back yard; I was hooked. I had finally gotten the dog I'd always wanted!

I put Condor in my car, and after I'd turned my tip bag in for the night, proceeded to drive my new friend home. Hmmm. A dog's gotta eat, right? OK. I stopped at the 7-11 & bought him the biggest can of Alpo I could find. I just loved looking out the store window & seeing him there on the front seat, waiting for his master like a good pal.

Everyone was already asleep when I got home, so I just led Condor into the back yard. I got one of Mom's bowls out & plopped the Alpo down for my buddy. He gulped it down in about 3 swallows and looked at me & smiled 'That was a good snack. Got any more?' I promised myself I'd get him more in the morning, said Goodnight, Condor, & went to bed.

Please note, earlier I said Condor had gotten hurt jumping over a 6-foot fence. It didn't occur to me that the 3-foot chain-link fence that lined my parent's back yard wasn't going to present him with much of a challenge. I also didn't consider what may happen if you take a dog away from its previous owner and abandon him in the back yard less than 3 hours later.

It was my mom that woke me up about an hour later.

"Mark?"

"Huh?" I answered intelligently.

"Mark, did you bring a dog home?"

I thought for a minute as the two moms in front of me crossed back into one. "Yeah, I did. His name is Condor."

"Well, you better come see. He bit a hole in the side door."

"A hole?" How does a dog bite a hole in a door?

When I got in the front room, my sister Cathy and mom were both up and walking around excitedly. My sister wore a laughing smile as she turned from the window.

"Is that your dog, Mark?"

"Yeah. Where is he?"

"He's in the back yard again," Cathy answered. "Boy, he sure is big. At first I thought it was a wolf!"

I looked out the window. Condor met me nose-to-nose through the glass, then opened his mouth, BIT the screen & pulled it out of the window & dumped it on the ground. He then got up on his hind legs and jumped excitedly, with his big black nose making snot blots on the window.

"He sure does like you," my mom said, shaking her head in disbelief.

"How'd you know he was here?" I asked.

"I was walking through the living room, going to the kitchen to get a drink of water," Cathy explained. "I heard a noise in the back yard, so I looked out the window & WOAH!" She jerks her head back in reliving the experience. "He's scary-looking!"

"Yeah, he is," I said with pride. My dog. My big monster dog. "You said he did something to the door?" I asked Mom.

"Yes, he did!" Mom answered with amazement. "I never thought a dog could eat through a door, but he did. He must've seen you go in the garage after you left him in the back yard. You want to see?"

"Sure," I said as we headed for the garage.

Mom opened the side door up, and there was the proof. Little splinters of door littered the sidewalk. He had managed to get through the outside of the hollow door, and made a hole in it you could fit your head in, but he stopped shy of punching his way all the way through. What a dog!

"Wow." I said non-chalantly. "He almost made it through."

My mom was a little less impressed than I was. "What are we going to do?" she mused worriedly. "We can't keep a big dog like that."

Why not, I thought. What's the big deal? You put him in the back yard, and you go pet him every once in awhile, or go wrestle him, or take him for a walk. At least, that's what I used to think before tonight. I had an idea.

"How about he stays in my room?"

Mom's eyes got bigger. "No! He can't stay in the house! Your father is going to flip out when he sees you brought a dog home. Please don't bring him into the house," she warned.

Time to kick the guilt machine on. "You think he'll make me get rid of it?" I said with sad, hurt, but still cool, eyes. "I've always wanted a dog."

"Well, I don't know," Mom replied, looking at the door. "Why don't we put him somewhere and I'll talk to your father in the morning."

"How about the garage?" I suggested. "He won't do anything in here."

"Well," Mom paused. Mom was easy. She let me do whatever I wanted. Dad was going to be the real trick. "I guess so," she said finally.

I went to the back yard, where my wolf-dog was waiting for me. He started whining impatiently as soon as he saw me. "Come, on, boy, let's go in the garage." I opened the gate & Condor pranced through. Mom & Cathy took a step back.

Cathy said, "Don't you have a leash for him?"

"Oh, yeah, I forget where I put it," I answered, not concerned at all. I knew Condor was harmless. Unless you're a door, or a window screen, that is. Or another dog.

I put Condor in the garage, said good-nite & closed the door. He immediately began whining and whimpering. I opened the door. "Condor, stop it!" He just looked up at me with that big, smiling face. "Don't do that any more!" I close the door. He starts in again. I open the door. "Condor!" I'm not yelling; just sort of whispering loudly. The last thing I need to do is wake my dad up. Condor just sits there & pants. I close the door. More whining. I suddenly realize that I'm tired and I need my rest.

I give my mom instructions. "Just leave him in there for awhile; he'll stop." (Yeah, like I know what I'm talking about. I've never been with a dog more than 5 minutes to pet one over the fence before.) And with that, I retired for the evening.

Mom didn't get much sleep that night. In the morning, I found out Condor had whined all night long, and Mom had tried to console him, although she was too scared to open the garage door all the way. She'd peek her head in the crack & whisper, "Condor, it's ok. It's OK, boy." And Condor had jumped up on the garage door leading to the house. To this day, that door is covered with deep nail scratches from that night.

The next day, I took Condor with me to the pet store for the biggest bag of dog food I could find, then I went to the pizza place to pick up my check. I left Condor in the car with the windows open a little while I went inside.

A few minutes later, Craig rushes inside. "Mark, is that your dog out there? That big brown one?"

"Yeah," I answered.

"He's honking the horn on your car!"

"What? You're full of it, Craig." Dogs don't do that. They sit and wait patiently for you to return, like an obedient servant.

"No, I'm serious, man. Come and see! He's sitting in your car with his paws on the wheel, blowin' the horn!"

Well, I didn't actually get to hear him honking the horn, but he had moved from the back seat to the driver's seat, and had painted the driver's door window with a thick coat of snot & drool. When I got closer, I noticed that the back seat was no longer in one piece, but had been split apart at the seam & all the foam was poking out, and my seat belt no longer had a shoulder strap, but a tattered fragment swung from the shoulder hook. Condor just looked at me, smiled & drooled.

"Condor!" I yelled, at once angry and impressed.

Craig was still in shock. "Did that dog eat your seatbelt?" He looked in the car again. "Was your seat like that before? Did that dog do that?"

"Yeah," I said, letting him out on the ground. He was smiling and happy as ever, wagging his tail and looking up at me. How could I be mad at a face like that? What's a couple of hundred dollars in damage between friends anyway?

Well, Kate heard about it and the next day offered to take Condor back. I refused, of course. She pointed out that in 24 hours, Condor had escaped out of the back yard, destroyed a door, ruined my seat and ate my seatbelt. Maybe he's just too much. I said no way, he's my dog, no matter what. I was very loyal. Dumb, maybe, but loyal.

But not as loyal as Condor was. His happy personality eventually even won my dad over. Everybody loved Condor, and Condor loved everybody else. Except other dogs, of course. You'd better have two hands on that steel cord leash when a poodle comes into sight. I used to double up the leash & wrap it several times around my arm, and hook both ends back into his collar.

He sure seemed healthy, but his first visit to the vet revealed he had heartworms, and lots of them. The vet only offered me a 70% chance he'd recover, at a cost of over $200 for the treatment. Add that to the cost of a new door, rear seat & seatbelt, not to mention the 50lb bags of food, and this was beginning to be an expensive venture of mine. But, what could I do? Love knows no spending limits.

I took him down to the vet for is heartworm treatment, and they kept him a few days. He was pretty lethargic when he came back, and it took a few months before he was up to his old strength. He never caused a problem before that, always minded his own business in the garage, except for that one time he got diarrhea and more or less blew up. Man, there was poop & barf everywhere. But after he recovered from the heartworms, he got a lot stronger. My mom couldn't handle him any more, and I wasn't home enough, so eventually I had to give him away to this ranch/kennel place I found. It sure was sad to see him go, but I think he's happy now. They train police dogs there, so they knew how to handle a giant baby like Condor. I went back to see him one time, and he just stood there and panted & smiled like no big deal.

That was a very, very good dog.

Chapter 20:   Life With Kate

I think Kate liked me. I think I liked her, even though she was not quite my type. I didn't know what my type was. I figured, hmmm, voluptuous, skinny, kind, gentle, smart, adoring, patient, exciting, loyal and forgiving, with red hair and just a few freckles, and a love of everything I like, totally selfless and never complaining. Too bad. Kate was short.

Everyone seemed to be in competition for Kate. Peter was. Found out he scored with her, at least once. (Boy that brought my respect for her down. Surely she could do better than a delinquent transvestite!) And Brian liked her. So did Terry. One time we were there outside Kate's house. Everyone was smiling and talking to the girl; me, Terry & Peter. She just smiled back, going from face to face to make sure we all got a little attention. Just lapping it up like a thirsty poodle. But I know Kate liked me. I mean, she baked me a cake and everything. Of course, my mom had, too. And I felt like I should at least TRY to eat them both. And I thought chocolate cake would go quite well with some whiskey from my collection of Jack Daniels whiskey bottles hidden in my closet. Oh, and did I mention that I got a little sick? Kind of like, throwing up chunks of alcoholic cake and heaving until my stomach ached and my sister asked my mom, Is Mark dying? And then my mom decided what she needed to do was spray down the toilet with extra-strength Lysol disinfectant, which I got a good lungful of on my next session in the bathroom. Talk about ralphing. I got so red I thought my head was going to explode! After a few violent (but germ-free) upheavals where my body attempted to expel several internal organs, I started to wish it HAD exploded. To this day, I never get drunk and eat two chocolate cakes on the same night. I learned my lesson.

I ended up driving Kate around one time. We stopped at the lake, and were just lying back in the seats, looking at the moon. I wanted to. I had opportunity. I wasn't inexperienced. I mean, she was RIGHT THERE and everything. But something wasn't right. Darn Catholic conscience. Stupid nerd timidity. I remember crying & praying after she fell asleep on my chest. God, I don't deserve this. I don't deserve someone to love me. I need it, I want it, I'm so empty inside. And eventually, the sun came up & I drove her home. (Told ya I was weird.)

Terry ended up "winning" Kate. He got an apartment and they moved in together. Terry was a plump, stout kid you'd probably see in the lunchroom eating 3 sandwiches and talking about how he pounded that linebacker at the last game. He wasn't violent, as far as I knew then, but he was scary-lookin'. He talked big, he was big, and he drove a truck that made small sedans look like speed bumps. Like a big teddy bear, but one that karate-chops. Just don't get him mad. One of his favorite hobbies was torturing fleas. One time when I was visiting them, Terry picked something off his skin.

"Is that another flea?" Kate asked worriedly.

"Yeah, sure is," Terry replied and headed for the stove.

Kate just shook her head. "We need to get an exterminator."

"Why?" Terry asked from the kitchen. A minute later there was this minute little pop! and Terry started laughing. "Got him!"

"What'd ya do?" I asked.

Kate responded while Terry turned off the stove but continued snickering. "He puts the fleas on the stove & watches them explode."

"Yeah," he confirmed. "It's the only way to kill 'em. They're tough little boogers."

They sort of adopted Peter. He was like their little kid. They'd tell him not to do this, stay out of my stuff, be home at this time. Terry had told him several times to stop borrowing Kate's car. He did anyway, and Terry saw him. Peter in the little Chevette, terry in his monster truck with his bright lights on. When they got home, Peter puts on his little-kid puppy-dog smile & says "Sorry Daddy" – I mean, he said "Sorry Terry". So nobody got a bloody nose or anything. I swear, that guy gets away with murder! Nobody can be mad at him! He could charm a Grisly. He'd go kick a cub, get the mama bear all angry, and five minutes later they'd be sittin' on the beach sharing a salmon.

After Peter freaked out & went to the loony bin, I kind of lost touch with them. I did get a phone call from Kate about a year later.

"Hi, Mark," came her small little voice.

"Hi, Kate. How are you?"

"I'm fine. How are you doing?" She sounded sad. What's up with that?

"I'm ok." Something must be wrong. "How's Terry?"

"Oh, he's not here right now. He's OK." The dip in her tone told me Terry was NOT just OK.

"Are you two still getting along OK?" I prodded.

"Yeah…" She broke off her sentence. I could tell she was trying to control her tears.

"He's not hitting you, is he, Kate?" That was instinct. I hadn't seen either one of them for months, but I just knew what it was.

"Well, maybe," came her sheepish reply. "It's not that bad, really."

"So he HAS been hitting you? Kate, that's terrible! What are you going to do?"

"Well, he doesn't do it any more. He just gets real mad sometimes. You know."

I did know. Terry's bad side is a good place to have life insurance.

"Kate, you've got to get out of there. No one should be hitting you like that. You're a good person." That jerk! If he weren't twice my size and ten times as tough, I'd ….

After a sniffle or two, she replies, "It'll be OK. If he does it again, I'll leave for sure." Yeah, right. I believe that. I believe he's not manipulating you and abusing you and you're not the trusting, naïve type to keep forgiving him over & over. And he's really changed now. For no apparent reason, he's going to just start automatically gaining control over his temper, and not get mad any more or hit you any more because he was SOOO sorry he did it last time.

How do girls like this survive?

After a few more words, we said our goodbyes & hung up. I'd really like to find out what ever happened to them two. I'd like to hear that Terry got stabbed in a bar fight and died instantly, while Kate went back to school, became a teacher, won the lottery and inherited 3 billion dollars from her newly discovered Great Aunt Queen Elizabeth. Now THAT would be fair.

Chapter 21:   Does That Hurt?

The time finally came for Kellie. It had been a long since our first meeting, and we'd been getting closer. The pregnancy was taking a bit more out of her than I thought it would. I mean, girls are supposed to gain weight, but I mean, geeeooollly, not that much! And aren't you still supposed to be able to walk? We had enjoyed spending some time together, going to the mall, just hanging around. I tried to take her to the local park. Figured we'd walk out on the pier, then go feed the ducks, maybe hang out at the playground.

Didn't work out. First of all, on the way there something fell off my car. I was just driving along, trying to act cool and not worry about the noises coming from under the hood, when there was this CLANG BANG CLANG as something rattled out of the engine bay, and then a PING Ping ping as it bounced along the road behind us.

"What was that?" Kellie asked.

"I don't know," I replied as I watched the car behind me get in the other lane. "I guess I better stop & see what it is." I pulled over & walked a few dozen feet to pick up my air conditioning pulley. Now how'd that get loose?

"It's nothin'," I replied non-challantly, as if this kind of thing happened all the time. "You still want to go to the park?"

"Sure, but I may not be able to do too much." That's OK. I just wanted to sit, talk, maybe make out. Getting a girl alone on a romantic pier, watching the birds fly over the water, casting long shadows as they fly by the setting sun sounded like a good way to blow an evening.

I pulled into a parking spot, got out & locked my door to make sure no-one would be able to steal my beautiful white chariot, and came around to help her out.

"Can you give me a little help?" She extended her hand.

"Yeah, sure." She lifted herself and big belly ball out of my car & I secured her door. She looked around. "Where do you want to go?"

I replied, "How 'bout over there? There's a nice little walk we can go on." I felt so big. Older, wiser Mark taking his little – uh, his big, pregnant girlfriend to the park he knows so well & showing her around. This was going to be fun.

Kellie nodded her head. "OK, sure," and we started off in that direction. I stayed by her side, holding her hand for support as we inched across the roadway.

"Slow down a little bit," she said.

"OK." I was getting a little concerned. It took us about five minutes to cross the park's street. I was thinking we might get mowed down by some motorist cruising along at the 5mph speed limit. I asked her, "Are you feeling OK?"

"Yeah, I'm OK," she assured me. "Just a little tired. Do you think we can sit down over there?" She pointed to a picnic bench about twenty feet away.

"Sure, whatever you want." I tried to prop her up as best I could, holding her arm like you'd do when helping your great-grandmother walk to the bed to get back in her oxygen tent. At long last, we made it to the picnic bench.

"I just need to sit here for awhile." She looked at me with a smile that seemed to say thanks & sorry about this at the same time. Boy, she's got a nice smile. I could get used to that face.

We sat. We talked. After about 20 minutes, she says, "Well, ready to go home now?"

Huh? You mean, that's it? No pier? No ducks? No romantic necking in front of the birds? What a ripoff. I want to see some tall weeds, and spiders, and have her put her head on my shoulder & say This was a great idea Mark; you're wonderful; give me a kiss, you wise romantic sexy guy you...

Not today. So, we shuffled back to the car & I drove her home. Maybe after the baby is born... which from the looks of her, would come any minute.

It wasn't long before Kellie called to say she was at the hospital. I went to visit her there, not knowing really what to expect. As I walked into the dark, quiet room, I saw her sitting on this big bed, with her dad sitting on a chair & her mom by her side. She had tubes coming out of her arms & was wearing a blue & white gown & covered with lots of blankets. There were actually quite a few people in the room. A nurse was bent down looking at some kind of chart. A couple of Kellie's friends were there, too. Andy was sitting on the bed. Lance was sitting backward in another chair, his chin on his hands and smiling stupidly. I never liked Lance. I'd met him once before and he hugged Kellie way too intently for "just a friend" status. I probably should've slugged him. Andy turned around & gave me a smile when I walked in.

"Hi, Mark!" Kellie said.

"Hi," I replied timidly. I hate walking into a room where everyone can see you. I suddenly felt the wish to be invisible. Too many people.

"I think you know everyone," Kellie continued. "You know Andy, and this Lance..."

I uttered a cool-sounding "Hey" in their general direction & found a free spot of wall to try to disappear into.

"Come over here, Mark," Kellie beckoned with her hand. Andy moved back a bit on the bed. I glided over there & took her hand.

"How are you feeling?"

"Oh, I'm OK. The contractions aren't coming very close together yet." The nurse looks up & gives me a smile before she goes back to her chart. Kellie's mom is smiling, too. So is her dad. In fact, everyone in the whole dang room is smiling all over the place. It was sick.

Then I remembered. "Oh, I brought you something," I mentioned as I bent down & reached in my sock. That was a trick I'd learned in Austin. You can hide things in your sock that would otherwise get squished in your pants pocket. I came back up with a nice big Snicker's bar. "Here you go! Thought you might be hungry."

"Oh, I'm sorry," she apologized. "I can't have any food while I'm in here." I could tell she really wanted the candy bar. Snicker's was her favorite.

"Oh, bummer," I replied as I tucked it back in my sock. I'd give it to her in a few minutes, after the baby comes. Kind of a celebration meal.

The doctor comes in with, you guessed it, a smile. She's a tough-looking Indian lady, looks like maybe in her 50's. Her smile quickly fades as she gets down to business. Something about labor not progressing, Petosin, induce; a whole lot of weird, new words. She leaves, the nurse leaves, then comes back with a shot & another bottle of clear liquid stuff to hang on a pole. From what I gathered, they were fixing to drown the baby because it didn't come out yet.

Well, things started happening. Most of the smiles went away. Kellie started to be in pain. She'd turn this way, then that. Her mother would try to put pillows in different places. And every few minutes, there was a "contraction", whatever that is, and her mom would stand at the foot of the bed & count with her fingers while whispering "hee hee hee whoo hee hee hee whoo". Kellie did the same hee-hoo thing with her mouth as she fixed her eyes on her mom like her life depended on it, all the while wearing an expression of wincing pain.

Gradually, the room cleared out as Kellie's lesser-devoted friends decided this wasn't as much fun as they thought it was going to be. I ended up on the bed, applying pressure to her lower back until MY back started to hurt.

"A little lower."

"Like this?"

"Yeah, but real hard." This was not romantic at all. Stroking Kellie's back was beginning to be real work. I was twisted all around trying to get some leverage. And she'd keep going into these episodes every couple of minutes, hee hoo hee hee hoo relax roll over deep breath say oh no sit straight pained expression look at mom hee hoo hee hee hoo fall back relax. All the while the nurse keeps adjusting this belt on her enormous round abdomen (it's too big to call a "belly") & you can hear this tiny heartbeat on a speaker, although it sounds more like it does when you use a squeezy bulb to squirt water in your ear than a heartbeat. I was stressed. For all I knew, this was the worst pregnancy in the history of the world, and my new girl friend was going to die, maybe this contraction, or maybe the next one is just going to do her in. How can a human survive such excruciating pain & torture?

After a few hours of this, off-and-on with having to leave the room for the doctor to examine Kellie, I was beat. I think I felt everything Kellie did but twice as bad, because I could only imagine how bad it really was. Then after one unusually long wait in the hall, the nurse called me in. "Mark? Are you Mark? Kellie wants you."

OK, now's when she says it. Mark, remember me as I was. I won't blame you if you decide to date after my funeral. Here, I want you to have this baby heartbeat monitor to remember me by.

"Hi, Mark, you can come in now," her dad told me. Nice guy. Big, friendly, couldn't hurt a flea. Of course, that's what I originally thought about Terry…

"Mark, you don't have to wait out there any more. We're just trying to decide something." She was sitting up a little more, and wiped her nose with a tissue once or twice. Her eyes were getting red from crying.

"What's the deal?" I was afraid to ask, but I did any way. Probably deciding on a burial plot.

They kind of ignored my question, but I got the gist of it. The baby wouldn't come out. It was late. Kellie had been there in the hospital all day. The doctor wanted to do a c-section, which is when they cut you open & take the baby out. Like when you slice a jelly donut instead of squeezing the jelly out of the hole. It doesn't seem like a big deal now, but Kellie really wanted to have a baby the natural way.

The doctor explained, "We try to give Petosin, but it not work very well. I think we should do c-section, or you might be in labor all night. That not good for the baby. Then I probably have to do c-section in the morning anyway." Dr. Ghandi apparently was trying to make a peaceful situation out of it, but her rough Indian charm wouldn't allow it. It came across to Kellie more like "I'm going to cut you up because you're going too slow."

But the reality of labor pains wasn't lost on Kellie. She was already pretty tired. She looked at her mom, who smiled & looked at her dad, who shrugged & looked at me. I looked at the ground.

The doctor said, "I leave you alone to decide. I'll be back in minute."

In the quiet room, with just me & the patient & the parents, they considered their options. Kellie was tearful but calmer. "I don't know how much more of this I can take."

"It's OK, Kellie," soothed her mom. "A c-section isn't that bad, is it?"

"What do you think, Dad?"

Her dad shrugged again. "I don't know. I think you should just do whatever the doctor says," he offered.

Kellie considered this & nodded her head. "OK, I guess I'll do it then. Go ahead & tell her."

"I'll get the doctor," I said, glad for a chance to do something helpful. I went down to the nurse's station & told her they'd decided, and she came in the room, said all kinds of technical stuff. Blah blah we have to shave you blah blah get you ready blah blah take off the Petosin blah blah about an hour blah blah anesthesiologist blah blah epidural blah blah blah. We were asked to leave as a couple of barbers came in. Outside the door I could hear Kellie crying as she was getting prepped for the O.R. Her dad didn't seem too terribly concerned, but I was a little uncomfortable. I felt like it wasn't my place to do what I really wanted to do, which was go in there, beat up the baby barbers, kick everybody out, and hold Kellie's hand & tell her everything was going to be all right. Whatever they were going to do, I'd just do it myself; pass me that knife & we'll get this thing done quick.

Later, I watched as they wheeled her bed down the hall. Her mom was dressed head-to-toe in a blue surgeon's gown, complete with blue sock things over her shoes and a blue hat. More people had arrived by then. Kellie's aunt, who was a med school student, was there, as well as the preacher from her parent's church.

I was getting really nervous. Oh, and I needed to take my pill. Good thing I have my pill bottle stuck here in my sock, right next to the celebration Snicker's. It was a migraine pill from my headache doctor. I had terrible migraine headaches. Bad enough to make you curl up into a ball in a dark room and pray for death. The pills seemed to be helping.

Understand that I was dressed in my usual rebellious teenager attire. I had a black concert jersey, extremely tight faded blue jeans, and extra-long hair that reached the middle of my back. With my big nose, my profile looks kind of like an afghan hound; you get the idea. I noticed Kellie's dad and preacher looking at me as I pulled a bottle of pills out of my sock. So, not wanting to be rude, I said, "Boy, I really need some speed. Anybody else want some?" They just sort of stared at me & shook their heads.

"No, thanks," came from the preacher.

"OK," I shrugged as I gulped down a couple of pills, showcasing my unique ability to swallow many objects at once with little or no water. After impressing everyone with my expert swallowing display, I non-challantly put the pills back into my sock and walked down the hall towards the door my girlfriend had gone through moments earlier.

There was a small rectangular window on the big double-doors, with a sign that said "No admittance". I peered through as best I could, but saw nothing. I then walked back to the other hallway, around the corner, and tried to catch a glimpse of her. Nothing. The family crowd was engaged in conversation by the waiting area. Small-talk. How have you been? How's work? Nice weather. Things at church OK? How's your husband?

I couldn't stand it. How can they just stand there & talk, when one of the nicest girls I ever met is being poked, prodded, drugged & sliced up? I decided to check the other hallway. Then I decided to check the first one again. No Kellie. I stood there for a minute, trying to make myself not care, just be cool and wait like everyone else. I couldn't do it. What's taking so long? I decided to check the hallways again. And again. I spent the next hour and a half walking back & forth, pacing & trying to see what they did with her.

Finally, after 1.7 eternities, I came around the corner & saw all the relatives plastered to the nursery window like a bunch of Garfield dolls. They were all smiling (ick!) and pointing. I walked over & tried to see what I could. There was a lady in there wearing a surgical gown. This tiny little baby was lying naked on a steel table, under a heat lamp & screaming so hard his face looked like it was going to pop. She didn't seem to even notice. She'd squeeze his hand, write something down, count his fingers, write something down – check, got 10 fingers, check, got 2 arms, check, got REAL good lungs. He especially liked the rectal thermometer, which the nurse mercilessly inserted into his tiny little butt while he complained with renewed vigor.

I lost interest quick. OK. So that tiny little creature came out of Kellie. Hard to believe. It must've been all hunched over in there to make a round stomach. But where was Kellie? Had she survived? Was she OK? What on earth was taking so dadgum long??? And then I saw here. She was alive all right. They wheeled her bed in the hallway and she was greeted by lots of How are you's & How was it's & He's so cute & I bet you're proud. I couldn't get very close to her with her aunt & uncle & cousins all congratulating her and her preacher and dad all saying how beautiful the baby was. I caught her eye as they wheeled her past. She smiled at me & that made me feel better. She was OK.

We all had to wait another hour or so while Kellie was in "recovery." Sounds like something an alcoholic should go through, doesn't it? Wonder if they're in there giving her hugs & saying I love you and following some 12-step plan to sobriety. I took turns between walking down to the recovery room to try & peak through the window, to going back & staring at the little baby. He had calmed down a bit, and they stopped irritating him. The nurse gave him a bottle – or more accurately, shoved it down his throat while he choked & gagged & tried to swallow – and put a diaper on him. He was tied up into a little cocoon with a blanket & put in a basket with his name on it. Baby Boy Brownd was his temporary name, since Kellie hadn't decided on a real name yet. I stared at him through the glass. He was kinda cute. His little bitty hand lay by his face as he drifted off to sleep. Poor little guy. He's had a rough day.

Kellie finally made it out of recovery. As they rolled her down the hall, I followed the crowd to her room and stood at the end of the bed (close as I could get) as she lay there. They brought the baby in his little basket & put him beside her. He was crying again. "Oh, poor baby," Kellie said as she tried to sit up. "Can someone give him to me?"

The nurse smiled & picked up the cocoon & nestled it by Kellie's side. He cried, pouted & then fell asleep as everyone went "Awwwwww, how cute." Kellie was about to fall asleep too.

"I can't keep my eyes open," she said. "Can I have some water or something? I'm real thirsty." Her brother Jody got her a cup of ice water, which she held in one hand as she tried to hold her head up with the other. Everyone was quiet, and smiling.

Someone asked, "What color are his eyes?"

She said, "Blue. They have to be blue, because both of his parents' eyes are blue." Suddenly, everyone in the room was staring at me. What? I'm not the dad. I guess they figured it out, because my eyes are brown. I was very uncomfortable. All these people staring at me, and thinking about that jerk that abandoned this sweet girl as soon as he ... I just kept my eyes on Kellie, and they eventually stopped looking at me. Great. Now I can't be inconspicuous, and at the same time I can't be involved. I'm an outsider, an unwelcome stranger. Perhaps I should leave.

Well, Kellie eventually fell asleep and everybody left. Her brother Jody got to hold the baby, and everyone just kind of stared at the little guy, and smiled, of course. I felt like I was invisible. What was I anyway? Not the father. Not family. Not even a close friend, really. Just a brown-eyed hippy with drugs in his sock. The only recognition I got was Kellie mouthed the words "thank you" to me before she drifted off to sleep. No one noticed. Everyone was talking to each other, the baby was asleep, Kellie was asleep, and it was nearly midnight. I left.

I was so mad. That was one of the most emotional things I've ever witnessed. I was drained. I had mentally gone through every contraction with her. I had paced nervously for hours. I hadn't eaten much all day, and I was tired. And where was Peter? Where was the little pr- uh, that un-nice person that caused all this? Who knows. Who cares. Good riddance. Stay away. Go die & burn in hell for all I care. Worthless pile of poop. I drove by & buzzed his house with my Camaro. It may have been a slow car, but with its V8, two-speed transmission, dual mufflers & several exhaust leaks, it was very loud. I think I even set off a car alarm or two as I raced by ScumSuckingJerkolaTerd's house. Wonder if anyone even noticed.

The next day was a little better. I went back up to the hospital. Kellie was awake, and we were alone for a bit. She let me hold the baby. Gosh, so little. We got to talk, and I helped her with her food when it came. I was smitten. I didn't know it then, but I was hooked. I think I really liked taking care of my little girlfriend and her baby. Something about it just seemed right.

Chapter 22:   Courtin' Kellie

Kellie wasn't really my girlfriend. I'd tried diligently to avoid that complication to my life. I was happy. I had a dog. I had a job. I had a car. I didn't have any responsibilities to speak of – not like a real adult does, anyway. There was the room in my parent's house, my Rush concert poster, my bass guitar. I could sleep until noon, stay out until dawn, and I owed nothing in rent and my mom did all my laundry. Who could ask for anything more?

By now, though, I'm sure you've figured out that I'm a sucker. I can't stay away from a warm smile or a pretty face. And it's all her fault. I'm not the one who smiled & talked & hung around so much. It's not me that put on makeup & sat there in the car looking so pretty & called on the phone for hours. I was an unwilling participant. I was coerced. I was forced by irrepressible enticement. She did it. She's guilty.

So, being under the bewitching spell of another female, I had no choice but to spend nearly every waking hour with her. I went in & out of that hospital so often they didn't even bother to ask my name. Oh, it's that hairy scary kid; just let him in, he's really harmless. I got to be by her side for at least 6 hours a day. Since she'd had a c-section, she was in the hospital recovering for quite a while.

I'd always come with a surprise up my sock. A candy bar. A big gumball from K-Mart. And I'd bring a deck of cards & play solitaire outside while the doctor came in & checked her plumbing.

One day, I was surprised to see my old pediatrician there. He was a nice guy, but I didn't really enjoy seeing him again. I mean, ever since I was old enough to remember, I'd gone to him for my annual checkups or the colds & allergies I always seemed to get as a child. Now when I meet him all I can think of is "turn your head and cough." But he was a nice guy, really. He said hi & we shook hands. Funny. I half-expected him to wash his hands afterwards.

Dr. RememberYouWhen turned out to be the baby's pediatrician. He went over to the baby with his stethoscope (the ice-cold skin-chiller model, if I remember correctly) & tongue depressor to examine little Baby Brownd. He poked & prodded, looked up his nose, in his ear, down his throat. Took off his diaper to check his motorworks, but I guess he was too little to know how to cough. I left to go get Kellie a coke or something, and when I got back he was gone. It wasn't until later that I found out what he'd told Kellie's dad while I was out. "You know that kid who was in here? Is he the father? He used to take drugs, you know. I'd be careful of him if I were you. I know. I was his pediatrician."

Isn't there a law against that? I have to hand it to her dad, though. He didn't judge me for it. He judged the doctor. You're not supposed to tell stuff like that. He didn't know me any more. I hadn't coughed in his office for years! What a jerk! I could have sued the indiscrete moron, if I weren't so anti-establishment in my nature. I mean, I could have sued him, or punched him in the nose! Yeah, or slashed his tires, or told his wife that I was his gay lover, or put x-lax in his coffee, or turned in an anonymous tip to the police about a pervert that just molested my girlfriend's new baby. But, like I said, Kellie's dad still liked me just fine. No worse, anyway.

Kellie had one nurse that I hated. She was a big, ugly, impatient witch from the 4th floor. Not normally on the maternity ward, she had no sympathy for anyone who complained of pain after something as minor as surgery. I know nurses are supposed to help, but sometimes you're better off if the battle axe just let you do it on your own. One time Kellie was trying to swing her legs out of the bed, to stand up and go to the bathroom. Every sudden move made her squeak in pain. Nurse Hitler didn't give a darn. "Come on, give me your hand."

"Ow! It hurts!"

"Just come on, get on your feet." SatanWoman gave her arm another tug.

"Aahhh! It hurts too much."

LuciferGirl just rolled her eyes. "It doesn't hurt that bad." But she did lay off a little bit. I wanted to deck the cold broad & beat her senseless. Instead, I just tried to burn a hole in her back with my laser glare. Didn't work.

Awhile later, we were trying to wrap the baby up after a diaper change. Kellie was exhausted & sitting in a chair. The baby was on the bed. I tried first this way, then that. Every time I did it, the blanket just came all undone. Finally I looked out the door for the evil nurse. "Can you come help us?" I asked.

With an irritated huff, she lumbered into our room & gasped. "Don't ever leave the baby on the bed like that!" She snatched the baby up. Chill, Nurse Grimsley. It's not like he's going to run away from home if we don't keep an eye on him.

"I was trying to wrap him up, but it just kept falling apart," I tried to explain.

"Well, let me show you how." I expected her to call me 'private' after that. She wrapped the blanket around, shoved it behind his back, wrapped the other one around, pulled it so tight I though I heard his ribs crack, tucked & shoved a little more and presented it to me for inspection. "There. Now that's how you do it."

"Oh," I said, enlightened. "I guess they're not as fragile as they look, are they?"

"Yes, you have to be very careful," she answered, missing my reply completely. "Never ever leave a baby alone on a bed like that. They could get hurt."

I resisted the urge to snap a salute & say "YES SIR!" Instead, I said "Thanks."

We had other problems with her. Most of the other nurses were real nice, but this one just had a "NOW what do you want?" attitude. I thought nurses were supposed to care for you, not boss you around & make you feel stupid. Like when Kellie was trying to get the baby to nurse. First thing, you know, after they're born, they get a nice big bottle of sugar water. That's before the mom ever gets to hold him. Then after that, they don't want milk. They want more sugar water. I was out of the room when she was trying, of course, but from what I hear, the nurse was like "Shove it in his mouth." "Put it in this way." "He's not taking it." "You're just not going to be able to breast feed." "We're going to have to give him a bottle if he doesn't start eating soon."

I can't see forcing such a little thing to eat every two hours. Poor little guy was just always, always tired. Kellie ended up having to wipe his face with a face rag. Wake up startled, sucky sucky sucky, stop, roll eyes back in head, drift off to sleep. Cold face rag, wake up startled, sucky sucky sucky, fall asleep again, etc. etc. etc.

I was as nervous as a dad when the time to leave the hospital came. We had talked about what she wanted to name the baby. The nurse came in to kind of send everybody off. This was the nice, smiling, good nurse. Here's the baby, see how the foot bracelet matches yours, so if we switched the babies then we switched the tags too, here's a bag of diapers & assorted trial-size baby stuff to take home with you, and have you thought of a name? Kellie smiled apologetically.

"Yeah, I think so." She looked at me. "I think we decided …" (she said 'we!' <giggle giggle>) "David Anthony Brownd."

"OK," said the nurse as she filled out the form, expertly balancing the baby in her left arm. "And the name of the father?"

I grimaced. Kellie suggested, "How about we leave it blank. Would that be OK?"

"Sure, no problem," the nurse scribbled away. I let a little sigh of relief out. I had gotten protective over these two people lately. The last thing that little innocent baby needed was his insane idiot scum bucket rat terd snot du-du brainless fartball father in his life. Then they put the baby – I mean, David - back in his little plastic bed & wheeled him down the hall as we scooted Kellie along in her wheelchair. That was just fine with me because I still felt pain when Kellie walked. It might be weeks before we got better.

Kellie's mom & dad brought their little economy car around the front of the hospital. Balloons, flowers, a suitcase & some pillows made their way into the front seat. A brand-new baby seat was in the back. They strapped little David in, and I stood there & watched as he squinted in the sun & disappeared down the street. I wanted to wave, but that wouldn't have been the cool thing to do. Sheesh. Before you know it, I'm going to be saying Oochi coochi coo.

Baby David didn't hamper our budding relationship. If anything, it started to bring us closer. I'd go pick them up, bring 'em over to my mom's house, and just hang around, watching him eat, throwing him up in the air. As it turned out, David had something called Colic. Nasty disease. It's this thing where you just scream your head off unless somebody is driving you in a car or simultaneously bouncing, spinning and patting you. I got a real workout. He also seemed to like stroller rides. I'd race him around the front room, making deeper & deeper ruts in the carpet, round and round. He loved it. Then I stopped. Waaaaah! Waaaaah!

Our "dates", if you want to call them that, also involved David. We'd take him around in my Plymouth (the Camaro rarely if ever ran), and talk as he slept in the back seat. Then just when he was out like a light, I'd pull into a parking lot or at a back road away from traffic, unbuckle my seat belt, slide over to my girlfriend's side, put my arm around her, and then … Waaaaaah! Waaaaah! Start the car up, drive around, slower & slower, park, try again … Waaaaah! Waaaaah!

I finally gave in to temptation and started thinking of her as my girlfriend. I know, I know. It's written right across my forehead. SUCKER! I even told her I loved her. I did. I really did. I had never been with a girl that made me feel so at ease, so comfortable, and a little excited at the same time. Dino wasn't that type of girl for sure – if you actually classify her as human. I don't know – are demon witches a member of the homo sapiens species, or are they considered non-living, or "undead"?

Before I totally gave in, though, I wanted to test her out. What does she think about me? Do you think she'd get jealous if I asked her about another girl? Would she react like my friend & be happy for me, or would she act like a girlfriend & get upset? So, I tried what has to be the oldest trick in the book.

"Hey, I wanted to ask you something."

"Yeah, what?" She turned to me with those big grayish bluish kindof teal eyes, the sunlight dancing off her hair in the summer sun. We were on the way to the mall in my car. Part of my plan. If we were facing each other, I don't think I could have pulled it off. I'm a terrible, terrible liar.

"Well," I started, trying to sound non-challant, "There's this girl that I kindof like a lot, and we're good friends and all, but I don't know if I should tell her that I really like her." I stole a glance as I turned into the parking lot. She's not buyin' it. "I met her at the mall a few times." There. A little detail to throw her off.

"Well," Kellie said carefully, "if you really like her, you should tell her."

"But I'm worried that we won't be friends any more." I was trying so hard not to crack a smile. I concentrated on finding just the right parking space. "I mean, she's a real cool friend, and I don't want to lose that."

"Well, if she's really a friend, then you can talk to her about anything." I looked at Kellie. Darn. She's a better liar than I am. Not a clue. If she's upset, she's hiding it well.

"So, you think I should just tell her how I feel?"

Kellie's response was, "Sure, why not?" Friendly and neutral. Not a hint of jealousy that I could tell. "If she says she doesn't want to be your girlfriend, and gets mad or whatever, she wasn't your friend to begin with." I detected the faintest tone of disappointment in her voice, but I couldn't be sure.

I took her up on that advice a couple of days later. I tried, tried so hard not to be nervous. I mean, I was old & wise, nearly 20 years old. I'd lived with a girl before. I wasn't new to this relationship thing. And Kellie? She was only 18. Would've still been in high school if they hadn't kicked her out. But, I got nervous anyway. I was driving her around. David was being baby-sat by Gramma. I'd stop. I'd turn. I'd say something stupid like, "On a scale of 1 to 10, how pretty do you think I think you are?"

"I dunno."

"Ten."

Silence. She smiled, though.

"Uh…. Let's drive somewhere else. You wanna go to the park?"

Ok, Mark, I said to myself. This is dumb. You've got to come up with a better line than that. What are you, a preteen inexperienced nerd? OK. This time kiss her. Yeah. Give her a big kiss.

So we stopped, I said something else really intelligent like "I like you a lot" and "you're nice".

I gave up. "I'm sorry Kellie. I'm not very good at this sort of thing."

"That's OK, Mark." She smiled.

"I never did like all that dating stuff. I just think you're great, that's all. I just like being with you."

"I like being with you too, Mark." Something about hearing her say my name made me all woobly inside. We stared at each other. I could stare into her eyes all day. As we were locked together in that moment, time just seemed to stop. It was her and me; there wasn't anybody else in the whole world except for us.

You might think we kissed right then, and maybe I should have tried. But, I was happy just to be with her; just to share a bench seat with this girl that made me feel so happy inside was enough for me. Sure we kissed later. After a couple of weeks, we held hands. Couple weeks later, we were laying on my bed together, playing with a microphone & being silly, when our eyes locked together & it just sort of happened. Kind of like slow motion, you know? We slowly, slowly leaned towards each other until our lips met. <Shiver!> Still gives me goose bumps thinkin' about it.

But from that moment in the car, I knew. She was my girl and I was her guy. Boyfriend and girlfriend, dadgumit. Maybe I'm a sucker, but I was with a really good girl this time. And this time, this sucker's going to stick. Just like movie theater candy to new shoes.

Chapter 23:   You did WHAT?

"Does that make you mad?" Kellie asked me timidly over the phone.

"Well, no." I had to think fast. Jeez. What am I going to do? I didn't expect this at all. "When did this happen?" I wanted to know.

"This morning at church," she replied. There was silence over the phone for a few seconds. "Mark, are you OK?"

"Yeah, I'm fine," I lied. This was great. Just great. Things were finally going well for me. I got rid of my demon-possessed girl/witch/Satan-friend, I had a dog, I had a car to work on that was COOL, and I had a girlfriend to come over & keep me company. I enjoyed my cigarettes. I enjoyed my closet full of whiskey, and my heavy-metal music, and I was looking forward to the next step there with Kellie, if you know what I mean. Just because we were going slow doesn't mean I didn't want to get there. And now THIS.

Here's what happened. Kellie had been going to church. I knew this. Of course, I knew all about church. You go, you sing, you sit & stand & kneel when they tell you, you suffer uncomfortably in dressy clothes for an hour, then you go home & celebrate having your freedom back. It was one hour a week, that's it. You go, you suffer, you leave.

But Kellie's church was different.

At Kellie's church, you go in & people actually talk to you. The first time I went with her to church, I strategically planned to carry David. It made for a good conversation piece, you know, or maybe just a shield or a decoy. Don't look at me, and if you do, look at the baby instead, isn't he cute? People talked to me anyway. I was sure I'd be left alone like I was at the Catholic Church. And I refused to dress up like I used to, so I wasn't looking like a saint, either. Didn't matter to those people. Oh, David got all the ohhs and ahhs you'd expect, but I got a lot of handshakes from people that at least seemed genuine.

The preacher must've remembered me from the hospital (hey, anybody want some speed?), but he didn't seem to hold it against me. "Hello, Mark. Glad you could make it." He smiled & shook my hand like a lumber jack.

"Uh, hi," was all I replied with, after he released the jaws of death from my crushed palm. I really didn't want to get involved with these people. I was just there because Kellie wanted to go, and I wanted to be with Kellie. I must've shaken about a dozen hands, and there weren't more than about 15 people there. Even the children were looking at me & smiling. Everybody was so happy. It was weird.

Then, when the services started, instead of a solemn procession of robed clergy, the pastor – yes, the pastor – gets an acoustic guitar on & starts playing! They sing some funky tune about He's Able & some other more serious thing involving blood. I kind of liked that one. A river of blood flowing out of Emmanuel's veins, pooling up in a puddle, taking a bath in it, wash away all your dirt, or something like that. Sure was different.

Then instead of the short, meaningless drudgery that I was used to from the priests – things like "God is like Coke; he's the real thing" – the pastor puts the guitar away, gets up behind the podium, and starts talking, zipping from bible verse to bible verse, getting louder & more excited. He was starting to work up a sweat, and he was meeting your eyes all the time. "It DOES matter what you believe." Was he looking at me? Why me? "Jesus loves YOU." I swear, the whole time, I thought he was preaching right at little ole me, the hippy in the back row holding a baby. And every once in a while, someone would say "Amen!" real loud. That'd just make the preacher more excited. He'd get louder, and louder, and more & more excited.

Finally, he'd quiet down & give what they called the "invitation". He'd say "Jesus is giving you a chance right now. Just come down here, and do what you know he wants you to do. Come to the front and I'll pray for you." A lady on the piano started tinkling some soft music as everyone – except cool people like me & David, of course – sang along, out of a big green book of music. That was another thing. Everyone did everything. When the preacher said, turn to John 3:16, everybody did it! Heck, we didn't even BRING our bibles to Catholic church! I thought reading the bible was a penance – something you do that hurts, so God won't be mad at you. Like giving up sandwiches for Lent. And during the invitation, a couple of men went to the front & kneeled down. How embarrassing. I felt bad for them. They were obviously upset about something. But everyone else just kept singing & singing, until those guys came back, wiping their eyes & rubbing their noses. And then it was over.

With Kellie's friends finding no time for her, and the school kicking her out before her belly started to show, she was spending more & more time at church. Not only did they go there on Sunday mornings, but Sunday nights, too, and even Wednesday's! And if you can believe it, they even do stuff on other nights, too, and have picnics & these "fellowships" where everyone brings a bunch of food & they all pig out & talk to each other. Wednesday's were real interesting for me. I hardly ever went – I mean, gosh, just Sunday morning was TWICE the hour-a-week punishment that I was used to – but they had this thing called Awana's, which is a ton of little kids, all running around this circle thing in the parking lot, throwing beanbags at bowling pins, walking like a crab, backwards. Then they'd go into rooms & study their little handbooks, memorizing stuff out of the bible to get more points, and at the end, they'd all come together & sing & get ribbons. Man, they could yell. And this was OK with everyone! It was wild! I mean, sure, it didn't look much like a church – a bunch of folding chairs in an abandoned shopping center and not a stained glass window or statue in sight – but still, I figured it must be a sin to shout in church, right?

After a few visits, I had gotten the gist of what they thought over there. Basically, they think everyone is a total hopeless sinner from hell, and everyone on the whole planet is going to go straight back there when they die, except for a few people who are "saved". I guessed it was just that little group in that church, and you had to not drink or smoke or have fun or do anything bad for you, except eat casseroles and brisket and cookies until you bust, that was OK. And when Kellie called me on the phone to say she got "saved", I knew what it meant. It was the end of our relationship, that's what it was. I wasn't about to give up my cigarettes and whiskey and cussing and heavy metal music. I was fine, I was happy with my life. No wonder Catholics always hate Baptists. You can do whatever you want when you're a Catholic; God was like Santa Claus. How many of us have been naughty instead of nice and STILL gotten presents Christmas day? It was going to be the same darn thing in Heaven. Everybody was going to get to go, in the end. The only people in Hell would be Satan, Hitler and my old girlfriend.

"So," I spoke into the phone carefully, "you really believe this stuff."

"Uh-hu." She sounded apologetic.

"So, how did it happen?"

"Well," she started slowly, "you know how I've been saying I like what the Bible says about family?"

"Yeah," I replied. Sure I did. The bible was apparently full of stuff about how the man is the boss and women should be submissive. I thought that was cool. I liked it when the preacher pointed his finger at all the women & told them they're supposed to let their husbands lead. I could handle that. I had already been fantasizing about how I could marry Kellie, and command her to shut the door, and unbutton her ...

"Well, I was thinking about that, and I went up to the front during the invitation." She paused, trying to find the right words to explain it. "And he told me, I need to believe in Jesus. I told him, I don't know about that, but I do believe this book; you know, the bible."

"OK." I braced myself for the rest of the story as I was building resolve to put this preacher guy out of business. This so-called pastor was looking more & more like a cult leader to me, praying on the naivety of a poor defenseless girl...

"And the he read this verse in John to me," Kellie continued. "It says, 'In the beginning was the word', and 'the word was made flesh' and stuff. So the bible is, like, Jesus."

"And then you …"

"Well, I just trusted him."

And then there was silence.

"Mark?" asked the small voice on the other end of the telephone.

"Yeah…" I replied.

"You OK?"

"Uh, sure, yeah." OK? Hell, no! My nice, fun girlfriend just turned into an uptight, judgmental Baptist! I was trying to decide if this meant dumping her, or if there was any other way out of this when Kellie offered me an opportunity.

"I think I'm going to be taking a bible class soon. They want me to take it before I get baptized."

"You're going to get BAPTIZED?" I asked incredulously. "What for?"

"Well," she said, a bit taken aback by my sudden rage, "you're supposed to get baptized after you get saved. That's how you join the church."

I knew what baptism was. I was an expert on it. Got baptized myself when I was the tender age of 2 weeks. Got pictures to prove it. But I was acutely aware of what baptism meant for Kellie and me now. It was like signing a contract; like saying, I'm in this for good, no turning back, I'm going to look down my nose at you drinking, smoking sinners down there from my state of near perfection here on this altar. Me good guy now; you bad; stay away. I couldn't let that happen. She was too nice a girl.

I thought for a moment. I had an idea. "Can I take this class with you?"

"Sure, I guess so." She sounded surprised. "Do you really want to?"

"Sure I do. I want to find out what these knuckle-heads have been telling you."

"OK, great. I'll tell them you want to take the class too then."

"Fine." I hung up the phone. Darn those smiling bible cultists. Take my girlfriend away, will you? Well, they didn't have her yet. Vampires only had the first bite in her neck. I would take those classes, prove them wrong, and rescue my princess from the clutches of the evil bible dragon …

Chapter 24:   A New Hope

A long time ago in a galaxy far, far away …

SOUL WARS

[insert theme music here]

It is a period of theological war. Rebel bible cultists, striking from a secret church in an abandoned strip center, have won their first victory against the young and naive Kellie. During the battle, they used the plan of salvation to attack with the Church's ultimate weapon, the BIBLE, a large black book with enough power to destroy an entire life. Pursued by the church's sinister agents, Princess Kellie races to meet her true savior, custodian of the plan to save her from doom and restore freedom to the galaxy ….

Together we drove to my first Bible class. I arrived at the doorstep a little before 7pm. I held Kellie's hand as I prepared to meet the enemy. I rapped lightly on the door as I braced myself for my first enemy encounter.

"Hi, Kellie, how ya doin'?" came the deceptively cheerful greeting. He was a moderately tall man, with red hair and a bushy caterpillar mustache. He pushed the screen door open as he took her hand. "So glad you could make it. And this must be Mark?"

"Yeah, hi," I answered defensively. OK, he knows my name. That's not a bad thing. I can handle this jerk. Sure, he's all cheerful and nice now. Just wait until the sun goes down and he puts that black cape on and black cats start circling above him in the air. "Nice to meet you," I lied.

We came in to the entryway, and Mark – same name as me, I know; another trick of the Devil for sure – introduced me to his wife Ida & daughter Amy. Ida smiled excitedly as she came from the kitchen drying her hands on a towel. "Oh, Hi, Kellie," she said. "I'm so glad you could make it!"

"Hi, Ida!" Kellie said as they embraced. Girls are always doing that. I guess it was OK; just as long as it's only hugs to old ladies in aprons, I can deal with it. (What, me, jealous?) Then Kellie waved a "Hi" to Amy, who waved back a "Hello" as she stood like a shadow behind her mom. Pretty girl, about maybe 11 years old. Poor thing. Probably got her own set of fangs in the top dresser drawer.

"So, this is Mark?" Ida enquired.

Kellie turned to me. "Yep. This is him." I managed a weak smile and a half-hearted wave. I was trying to look cool, and probably looked more like an idiot, but you have to keep your wits about you or they'll sell you on their twisted religion. So, a little distance at this time was a good strategic move on my part. I didn't want to get sucked into their cult vortex.

For a few seconds, everybody just stood there smiling at each other, and then Sorcerer Mark led us to the dining room table. "Let's get started."

Bring it on, you rebel scum.

We sat down, with Satan on one side and me & Kellie on the other. Let the battle begin. Mark began his attack.

"OK, what we want to do with these lessons is look at the Bible through the eyes of God," Mark explained. "We believe that's the only way for anyone to really know what is right and wrong. For instance, you work on cars, don't you, Mark?"

"Yeah…" I replied. How'd he know that? Did he look in his crystal ball? Did he summon the spirit of a dead sorcerer? Did he plunge his invisible tentacles into the recesses of my brain, even now as I sat in his presence?!

"Kellie told me you're even going to school to become a mechanic, is that right?"

"Oh … yeah, I'm going to San Jac." San Jacinto was the local community college.

"Well, then, if I were to ask a dozen people, say, what the best way to rebuild an engine is, how many different answers do you think I'd get?"

"Well," I thought. Hmmm. I'd actually been a little frustrated with this myself. Shouldn't there be just one correct way to rebuild an engine? But everyone I talked to, even my instructors, each had their own ideas. "Several, probably," I answered honestly.

"Right. That's because man looks on the outward appearance, but God looks on the heart. Turn to 1 Samuel 16:7."

So I did. I opened up my trusty Catholic bible, the one my grandfather had given me, and started searching for First Samuel. It took me a little while to find it in that dusty old book, but I did. Mark read aloud as I followed along.

"But the LORD said unto Samuel, Look not on his countenance, or on the height of his stature; because I have refused him: for the LORD seeth not as man seeth; for man looketh on the outward appearance, but the LORD looketh on the heart."

OK, I could go with that. Sure. God's the big boss, he's all-knowing and all-powerful. That agreed well with my Bible, even though some of the words were different. What's "seeth"? Why don't they just say "see" or "sees"? Weird.

Mark went on. "So if we're going to look at the world the way God does, how do we know what God thinks?"

Ask the Pope, I was thinking, but I didn't say it. "Uh, read the Bible?" I offered.

"That's right. But how do we know for sure the Bible is the Word of God?"

Bible. Word of God. This was getting thick. I know I heard the answer to this in some Sunday School class years ago, but I was drawing a complete blank. What was it? … Couldn't make it out. I'd always just sort of known that the Bible was God's book. I remember my dad telling me a long, long time ago, what if God sees me after I die, and the first question he asks me is, did you read my book? Not long after that, I think, I had started reading my little Catholic Bible. Didn't understand much of it, but darned if I wasn't going to study for that test!

Mark didn't wait for an answer. "There are three reasons why we know the Bible is the Word of God," he said. "Construction, prophecies and Bible claims. First, let's look at the construction of the Bible."

He went on to explain that the Bible had one central theme, Jesus Christ, and was totally free of errors & conflicts, even though it had been written over a 1600 year period by over 40 different authors. I didn't know enough to argue a point with him, so I agreed, the only way for that to happen was if God had written it. He then went on to show me some prophecies, or stuff God said would happen that actually did happen. I knew only a couple, like there was supposed to be a virgin that would conceive and bear a son, and that would be Jesus. Everyone knows that one from the Christmas story. And then we went through some verses that said the Bible was not only inspired by God himself, but was actually useful for "doctrine, reproof and correction." Hmph. I always thought it was just a holy book you had to read & couldn't possible understand. Very interesting.

This wasn't what I had expected. I began to lower my guard a little bit. I mean, Mark didn't say two words without opening up the Bible and showing me at least one verse that said the same thing. I wonder why the Catholics never use the Bible like this? I've never had anyone try to dissect it before.

"And why is it important to know what God said in the Bible, Mark?" Mark asked.

I shrugged. "I guess because he's going to ask you some day, right?"

"That's right! Turn to Romans 14:11." I looked over at Kellie. She smiled as she squeezed my hand. Her eyes seemed to say, You're doing a good job, Mark. I didn't see the hypnotic glazed-over zombie stare I was expecting when she got around these cultists. In fact, I was beginning to reconsider if these were cultists after all. Maybe they just know how to read better.

I found the book of Romans without too much trouble:

For it is written, As I live, saith the Lord, every knee shall bow to me, and every tongue shall confess to God.

I knew about that, all right. One day, everyone in the world is going to go before the big white throne. God's going to take your life, and play it on a huge screen TV for everyone to see. And if you're lucky, you'll have more good things than bad things in there & you'll go to Heaven. If not, you'll go to Purgatory for awhile & suffer, until you've made amends. But if you're real bad, like you murdered somebody or something, you'll pass Purgatory and go directly to Hell. Whew! Good thing that doesn't apply to me. I mean, I've never murdered someone – oh, wait, I did. Uh-oh.

Mark goes on to show how the judgment is going to be according to "truth", and that God's Word is "truth." The lesson finishes up with how God divides the world up into two groups: those who have a relationship with him, and those who don't.

After a little chit-chat, thanks for coming, same time next week?, we leave. I had come there really intending to stand my ground against the onslaught of lies, deceit and trickery. As it turned out, I was presented with facts in an organized way, so I found out we were both standing on the same ground. So far, any way. I didn't know what those two "groups" Mark was talking about would be. Maybe there's the "whole world" on one side, and "our secret cult society" on the other. You can't get to Heaven unless you join our church and drink this cat blood and tattoo your eyeball with our insignia.

~~~~~~~~~~~~~~~~

The following lessons were pretty interesting. I kept waiting for Mark's evil laugh to surface as his head spins around & all the pictures on the wall fall off when the ground starts to shake & lighting flashes, but it never happened. Instead, each week we'd sit down, open our Bibles, and talk.

Lesson 2 was all about these two groups Mark had mentioned. In this column, we have all the lost people. They're lost. They're unrighteous. They're unforgiven. They're condemned. They're all just dirt bag skumbucket sinners headed straight to Hell. Then on this other column, there's the saved. They're righteous. They're forgiven. They're justified. They have eternal life and are headed straight to Heaven.

I never knew it was so simple. I tried to find an argument, but heck, how could I argue? He'd read a verse to make his point, then I'd see the same darn verse in my Catholic Grampa Bible. It all matched up perfectly, except for some "thou's" and "thine's" and other weird speech problems. The verses said the same thing, though. Maybe I should have brought a priest with me, but those guys give me the willies.

It all made sense and I was starting to suspect that I may not be in the column that I wanted to be in. He said, "Mark, if I were to tell you that right now, you're in this column here," as he pointed to the 'No Relationship' heading, "what would you do?"

I thought for a minute. "I guess I'd try to do something to get over here," I answered nervously, pointing at the other column. So much for me, the mighty soul warrior. I was scared that I actually WAS in that bad-guy category. I certainly didn't feel like I'd done enough to get over in that other column. Bet those guys over there never took drugs or cussed or ran away from home or stole a thing in their life.

"Well," Mark said. "Let's look at it. Suppose you decided to have 100% good conduct. You went to church, gave them a bunch of money, you helped the poor, helped your community. You did everything right."

"OK," I responded.

"Now, let's see what the Bible has to say about this. Turn to Ephesians 2, verses 8 & 9." This is what it said there:

For by grace are ye saved through faith; and that not of yourselves: it is the gift of God:

Not of works, lest any man should boast.

That "not of works" part kind of stuck out to me. "So, you're saying you can't get over here to this side by doing good stuff?"

Mark smiled like a teacher whose pupil was starting to grasp a concept. "That's right. Let's look at another one: Titus 3 verse 5."

Not by works of righteousness which we have done, but according to his mercy he saved us, by the washing of regeneration, and renewing of the Holy Ghost;

So, I was starting to get a little nervous. All my life, everything I had ever known about God & Heaven, may have been wrong. I'd always believed that, if you lead a good life, do your chores & homework, pay what you owe and give a little away, God would let you into Heaven. It was as simple as that. If you're good, you go up; if you're bad, you go down. Now it was looking like no matter WHAT you did, you were doomed.

Mark confirmed this for me. He said, "There's absolutely nothing you can do, Mark, to get yourself into this column here. And who do you think is in this column over here, and headed for an eternity in Hell?"

"Um, a lot of people?" I answered, trying to divert attention away from myself. Let's not talk about me. Let's just talk about 'lots of people.'

"Well, let me show you what it says in Romans 3:23." Once I found it, this is what it said:

For all have sinned, and come short of the glory of God;

"That means everybody; all have sinned. That means, you, me, Kellie. Everyone." I stared at the verse and tried to think of an argument, but couldn't come up with one. I mean, there it was, right in the Bible. Might as well have had my name on it. Romans 3:23: Mark sinned and everyone knows it, and when he dies, he's going straight to Hell.

And that was the end of THAT lesson. Pretty gloomy stuff. The next couple of lessons were a little more up-beat. Mark talked about how Jesus had come & died on the cross to pay the price for our sins. His death, burial & resurrection were all that were needed to move people from the "No Relationship" column to the "Relationship" column. We must've looked up a hundred verses that all talked about Jesus being a sacrificial lamb, about him being the Messiah.

By this time, I had long given up on the idea of defending Kellie from these people. I wish Mark had done something mean, or said something stupid, but dadgum it, every single thing he said came right out of Grampa's Bible! The only way I could've argued with him is if I'd denounced the Bible as a bunch of superstitious poppycock, but I was in enough trouble with The Big Man as it was. I wasn't about to bad-mouth his holy Word!

And finally the time came. It was toward the end of the fourth lesson. It's when the teacher switches from talking about "they" to talking about "you." Like an expert salesman, he convinces you that everyone in the world needs a compact, battery-powered veggie-matic processor, and then he says, "What about YOU, Mr. Smith? Have YOU got one of these little jewels in your cupboard?"

Mark moved slowly in for his tender kill. We looked up one last verse, John 3:36. He wrote the first half of that verse on the back of the chart he'd been filling in for 4 weeks.

He that believeth on the Son hath everlasting life

First we looked at that last part; "hath everlasting life". Translated into modern English, that would read "has everlasting life." Mark said, "That's God's part. He has promised to give eternal life to everyone that believes on him. If he didn't, then he'd be a liar, wouldn't he?"

I nodded dumbly, feeling too much on the spot to come up with a reply.

"Now, let's look at these other sections. That first word, 'He', that means anyone. It doesn't matter how bad you've been, or how old you are, man or woman, none of that matters. It's available to anyone."

"Uh-huh." Kellie squeezed my hand a little tighter. She could tell I was getting a little tense.

"And that second part," Mark continued. "That believeth. That word, believe, means trust. Whosoever puts their total trust in the Son. And we know already who the Son is, right?"

"Jesus," I answered, in a different kind of tone than I usually use for that word.

"OK, now I'm going to draw a line, and this line will represent your life, from birth until death." He draws this long line across the page, and puts 'birth' at the left end and 'death' at the right. Then he draws another line right before the 'death' side & labels it 'now.'

"Now," Mark said, reading my features & realizing that I wasn't too comfortable having my 'now' line so close to my 'death' line. "You may not like the fact that this line is so close to this line, but we know we're all going to die some day, and we never know when it's going to happen. It could be today, it could be tomorrow, or it may be 50 years from now. So let's just draw it there."

"OK," I replied weakly. It was starting to get hot in there. Was it just me?

"OK, I'm going to ask you a question. First of all, are you saved? Has there ever been a time in your life where you put your faith and trust in Jesus, and nothing else, to save you?" Mark's tone hadn't changed, but somehow those words seemed to almost sting as they hit my ears. I thought about the answer. Actually, I didn't. I was stalling for time. I pretended to ponder the question.

I knew. I knew instinctively that I wasn't saved. I knew what I had done in my lifetime. Nobody had to tell me I was a sinner. I was there. I had listened as I cussed at my parents. I had seen me stuff a new radio in my sock in the Target store bathroom. And I most of all remembered having a big part in the death of a small, innocent baby. I was guilty as guilty could get.

"No," came my weak reply. My palms were sweating. I lost all feeling in my feet. My heart was pounding in my ears. Here it comes, I said to myself.

"Well, then, you need to trust Jesus." I looked over and stole a quick glance of Kellie's concerned face. I went back to studying the paper in front of me. It sure was getting hot in there.

After what seemed to me to be a very long silence, Mark said, "Tell you what. Why don't we pray about it. I'll pray for you." So he did. I closed my eyes and tried to fight down the emotion that was welling up in my throat. "Dear Lord," he started, "This young man has come to realize that he's a sinner, and he needs to trust you. I know that you are a kind and loving God, and I pray that you would give Mark the courage he needs to trust you right now. I know that in your Word, you say that whosoever believes on you will be saved, and whoever comes to you, you will in no wise cast out. I pray that you would help Mark to trust you now, and believe in you, that you may wash his sins away and accept him into your family." Then he stopped. Everything stopped. I was alone in my thoughts, and nothing was going on around me. Everything was still and silent.

So I thought. I know I need to do this. I know I'm headed for Hell if I don't. But I just can't. I don't want to. No, I won't! I won't do this, not now, and maybe never! I don't want to get saved. I don't need to. I'll just be a good person, and it'll be ok. Forget it. I just won't do it!

Slowly, the panic started to leave me. I opened my eyes. Mark's eyes were still closed. I became aware that I had been squeezing Kellie's hand very, very hard. I sat up. Mark opened his eyes and looked at me. I just shook my head and gave an apologetic smile.

"I ... can't. I just can't."

Mark gave a little smile of his own. "That's OK. You don't have to right now." Kellie patted me on the shoulder. I was feeling a little more like myself. My hands felt very cold & clammy, but I could feel my toes again. My heart stopped racing and started to settle down to only 100 beats per minute. Everything was almost ok; almost back to normal.

We talked a little bit more, about what, I don't remember. I was just happy to be outside again where I could breathe. I welcomed the cool evening air outside, as it blew through my hair and brought some color back to my face. I drove Kellie home, as we talked about meaningless minutia. I told her good night, and she gave me a nice, long hug. And then I went home to be alone with my thoughts. Alone to wonder what it is that I actually believe. Alone to ponder if I really had the guts to let go of everything I ever trusted, and turn to something totally new. Alone to reflect on what I really am; and where I'm really headed.

Chapter 25: No, Luke; I Am Your Father

[insert theme music again, but louder this time]

It is a dark time for the Rebellion. Although the conviction from the bible class has been destroyed, Imperial Thought Droids have driven our hero from his hidden comfort zone and pursued him across the subdivision. Evading the dreaded Imperial Saving Faith, Mark has established a new secret base on the remote world of DontDoNuthin. The evil lord IaintGivinUp, obsessed with converting young Mark, has dispatched thousands of remote thought probes into the far reaches of the space between our hero's ears…

The scars from my battle were still on my soul as I headed to work at AutoZone. (Actually, it was called Auto Shack back then. That was before the Shack lawsuit made them change their name. I guess the guys at Radio Shack got just as tired of people asking for mufflers as we did people asking for radio's.) Boy, what a battle! I was still a little shaky. I'd come face to face with the evil Baptist Brainwasher Brigade, and I'd held my own! Barely, but I did. And I escaped almost unscathed with my Catholic beliefs and attitude. I was OK. I just needed to think for a little bit.

So, as I was straightening the Prestone Flush-N-Seal on the coolant aisle (one of my many important duties as Automotive Parts Technician), I went over it in my mind. You know, what has the Catholic faith gotten me so far? A lot of baggage, I'll tell you that. I felt guilty about stuff I did, sure. Doesn't everybody? But I didn't feel this forgiveness that everyone always says you have when you're religious. I was angry. That's it. I was just plain angry at God. How could God create a world so full of hate and jealousy and evil? How could he allow poor little pot-bellied babies to starve to death while flies buzz around their dirt cribs? (Hey, I know it's true – I saw that kid on TV!)

Who was I kidding… I was a loser. I deserved to go to Hell. I'd broken at least 8 out of 10 commandments. Years of training in the Catholic academy wasted. Once I had hit puberty, Bang! Right off the straight & narrow path & into the thorny bushes. I'd been bleeding ever since, with thorns sticking out of my skin like a Russian voodoo doll during the Cold War. I began to pray. Well, not pray. Maybe just talk in my head. I mean, I couldn't stop to kneel or anything – I was halfway to the radiator clamps, which by the way were embarrassingly disorganized.

I need to get saved. I don't understand this stuff that well, but I know what I know. Tryin' to be good ain't workin'. Maybe I will. Maybe at the next bible class. I dunno. If you even want me. I'll just do it. I'll just trust you instead of trying to do right. Just take me as I am, and I trust you to save me, Jesus.

[AAAAAAAAHHHHHHHHHhhhhhhhhhhhhh………... The shrill voice of the Evil Emperor echoes off the pit walls as our hero watches him descend out of site into the fiery bellows, never to be seen again]

Whoa! What a load came off at that moment! I felt free, so totally light. I even forgot about placing the Stant radiator cap in my hand back on the proper peg. I'd done it. Somehow, I don't know, I just – it was like – I was just free. I felt relief, like, Oh good, here's the bus, I don't have to walk any more. I can just let someone drive me home now. This was pretty cool. It was as if someone was there with me, like I wasn't alone…

And with a slight jolt I remembered where I was. I glanced around to see if anyone had noticed anything. I tried to shake off the euphoria and get back to work, but a little residual smile I think stayed with me for the rest of that day. And I began to think/pray/talk to myself like a crazy person. No, maybe I didn't do it right. I shouldn't have done it yet. I should have waited until I was with that Bible guy, what's his name – yeah, Mark. I should have waited. I probably messed it all up, like I do everything else. Yeah, you did mess it up, turkey. No, I didn't. Yes you did. Shut up. No you shut up. I'm not talking to myself. Yes I am. No I'm not. Stop it. Just do your job, AutoZone Man. I can do my job; you're the one with the problem. I don't have a problem. Yes I do. No I don't. Liar. Dummy. Poopoo head.

But, try as I might, my vain attempts at self-debasement met with little success. I was still feeling a little high on the relief when I went to see Kellie in the morning. No one else was up yet, and we were alone in the kitchen. I sat down across from her at the table. She smiled at me, with folded hands. The morning light from the sliding-glass door on the patio was making bright, long shadows in the room, and I could hear a bird chirping melodically outside. I took a deep breath as I looked into her eyes. Suddenly, I felt peaceful again. I think I could tell Kellie anything. She was so warm and understanding.

"Uh, there's something I wanted to talk to you about," I began.

"Yes, what is it?"

"Well, I think I might have gotten saved."

"Really?" Her eyes widened up a bit at the news. "What happened?"

"Well, I was at AutoZone yesterday, and I was thinking about what Mark said in the bible classes. And I think I trusted him. You know, Jesus."

A big, warm smile came over her face. "Really?"

I thought about it. This is it. Am I in or out? Whatever I'd done at work was still just a secret. I hadn't told a soul, not even my mom & dad. Well, that was nothing new, but still – this was my last chance to turn back. I took the plunge.

"Yeah, I did. I think I really did." I couldn't stop a smile from infecting my face as I felt that relief, that sense of security I'd had on the Coolant Aisle the day before come over me again. I realized right then, this was real. I was really a Christian now.

Kellie looked at me and smiled even more. "Mark, that's great!" And we just sat there staring at each other smiling like a couple of doped-up retards in the mental institution. I was so happy and secure right then I didn't even think about the enemies that I'd just created in my own house, right out of my own flesh and blood. People who had put up with every conceivable rebellious act this wicked teenager could think up. People who could forgive any bad behavior or evil deed, so long as I kept my good Catholic faith.

My PARENTS!

Chapter 26:   Return of the Believer

[insert theme music once more, but not so loud this time – oi, my head!]

Mr. New Believer has returned to his home in an attempt to rescue his parents from the clutches of the vile and empty Legalistic Religion. Little does Mr. NB know that the SUBURBAN PARENTS have secretly begun construction on a new weapon even more powerful than the first dreaded Religious Guilt Complex. When completed, this ultimate weapon will spell certain doom for the small seed of Truth struggling to restore freedom to our hero's soul…

"Hey, Dad, guess what?" I non-chalantly offer. I was in the kitchen. My dad was carrying a glass casserole dish back to the sink. My mom was busy washing a cup. It was a perfect opportunity to tell my parents both about this new faith I had in Jesus Christ. Kellie wasn't with me, which was actually pretty good for me. I needed to do this alone. All my life, I'd been dragged into church on Sundays to hear an old, wrinkled man in a robe talk about how we ought to be doing this, or ought to be doing that, when's the last time you stopped to look at a flower, you should be helping people more, put on a smile and lift someone's spirits, make someone's day. And I'd sit there and think about everything you could imagine, except what he said.

But that's not the point.

The point is, I had the truth now. I knew why I was never interested in God stuff before. I knew that what I learned was Truth, and what I'd been taught was a lie. I knew that no-one was going to go to Heaven just by doing those things that the priest said to do, because all they talked about was how to be good and give give give and guilt guilt guilt and Mary Mary Mary. I knew that the Bible was more than a sacred book to be respected. It was to be used. It had a message in it. And I had to tell my parents about my newfound revelation.

I'd gotten saved, all right. We had talked about it at the next bible class. I'd talked to the pastor at Kellie's church about it. Then one Sunday, during the invitation (that's when everybody stands up & sings a slow, soft song & the preacher calls for anybody to come to the front in case they need to pray or get baptized or whatever), I saw Kellie go forward. I knew why. She was going to get baptized. We'd talked about that too, at the bible class. First you get saved, then you get baptized; that's how you join your first church. Well, I wasn't about to be outdone by a GIRL, so I stepped out, too, and walked up to the front.

The preacher was happy to see me. He shook my hand and I told him I wanted to get baptized. Then I hugged him. Don't ask me why. I think it was a conditioned response. That's what everybody does at PDAP (Palmer Drug Abuse Program). They all say 'I love you' and hug you & say it's OK and you can do it. I'd gone there a few times with an old girlfriend. She had some serious mental problems; I guess we were a good match. Then I made the mistake of writing 'I love you' in her yearbook. I thought, hey, they said it at PDAP, it's no big deal, right? WRONG! She took the book back, stared at it, then tried to hug me. Hey, not now! I'm in the smoking area at school, and all the cool people can see me. So I wiggled free & told her, "Sorry. I've been feeling really weird today," as I stared blankly into space and took another puff. Well, that wasn't the last time I heard about THAT, I'll tell ya. She didn't actually confront me about it, but she got her friend Becky to do it. 'Mark, what did you mean when you wrote that in Wendy's book?' How could I tell her the truth? I didn't know what the heck that meant. I just thought she was cool, we both were messed-up druggie smokers, and I wanted to try it on for size. I babbled off some nonsense about it being a challenge to myself to see if I could overcome my frailties and rise to a new level of consciousness. She didn't buy it. I could read it in her eyes. 'Oh. So you lied.' Becky had good intuition. One time at the mall (she used to work at a video arcade), she told me I was a virgin. (She was right.) Darn intuition.

Anyway, this Sunday wasn't my first time to get baptized. I have pictures of my 2-week-old mess of red hair being sprinkled by a smiling old man in a priestly green and white gown. But this was different. This time, what you're trying to do is show how Jesus died, got buried & rose again. You need a lot more water to do that.

Preacher took Kellie & me & had us face everybody. He said, "These two have come forward for believer's baptism. All in favor say 'I'". They all said 'I' & smiled at us. Then someone gave me a white gown & told me to put it on. I went to the bathroom & changed into it, after Kellie was dressed & ready. Preacher got his hip waders on & met us behind the stage. Now, when I say this you say yes, then hold your nose like this & I'll let you down like this into the water, then you come back up. OK, let's do it.

The baptistery they had – that's the big tub full of water – totally dwarfed the one from my infant experience. It must have been 4 feet deep, and about 8 feet long. The preacher walked up the steps & into the water and motioned us to follow as the song leader brought the music to a halt. Then as I watched, he asked Kellie if she knew she had accepted Jesus as her savior. She said yes with a nod. Then he said, "By the power invested in me by Berean Baptist Church, I now baptize you my sister in the name of the father, the son and the holy ghost. Buried with him in baptism…" (This is where she held her nose & he let her down backwards into the water; it was just like a burial. I could see the water rushing in over her just like dirt over a coffin after being plunged into the ground; eerie.) "And raised in newness of life." Kellie came back up, blinked the water out of her eyes and smiled at the cheers of 'Amen!' of the congregation.

Then it was my turn. He asked me the same question, and I said yes of course, except then he called me his brother instead of his sister, and down & up I went. There were no camera flashes, and except for the small group of maybe 50 people gathered there in the unoccupied shopping center by the freeway, no one knew what happened. I felt like that made it even more permanent. Not to me, but to everyone else. I could now say I was a Baptist, and no longer a Catholic. I was officially a member of Berean Baptist Church, as I stood there dripping wet and looking out at all those smiling faces. Someone handed us towels as we climbed out of the earth-grave-water-pool, and Preacher had us both stand at the front as people came by & shook our hands. I got an especially strong welcome shake from Mark the bible class teacher, who was grinning enormously behind his thick mustache and red beard.

It felt good to belong.

So, I wasted little time in finding opportunity to articulate my experience to those happy parents from the wet redheaded baby picture. I had to be careful, though, as religion is such a deeply seated belief, especially for my parents. They were so spiritual they couldn't even talk about God & stuff unless something really scary was going on, like when my grampa was suddenly hospitalized with diabetes. I wanted to be gentle, but definitive; thorough but succinct; humble yet confident.

"Hey Dad, guess what?"

"What?"

"Me and Kellie got baptized!"

My mom's hands froze in mid-cup-cleaning as she stared at me. My dad put the casserole dish down and slowly turned to face me. I saw the same look of shocked disbelief in both of their stunned expressions. The silence was deafening. After what seemed like an eternity, I smiled and broke the icy chill with "Yeah, we're both Baptists now. Cool, huh?"

I could see the muscles tense up in my father's face. He didn't say anything, but if looks could kill, I'd be like roach guts on a fly swatter. With his shoulders hunched up around his ears and his angry gaze penetrating the linoleum, he just walked out of the room without a word and closed his bedroom door. My mom took it a little better. She shook her head as she finished wiping a mug clean and said, "Mark, that's terrible." I could feel the pain in her voice. "You're a Catholic. You were baptized when you were a little baby…"

Aha! Here's my first spiritual test! An infidel to convert! An unbeliever to enlighten! I will do my Christian duty and witness to this poor lost soul!

"Yeah, but that doesn't count. You have to get saved, and THEN you get baptized."

I waited for her to finish scrubbing that poor cup out some more. After she'd given it a few dozen more fierce passes with the sponge, she set it down and wrang her hands out on the dishtowel and shook her head again. "I don't know, Mark." She thought for a minute and gave me a sad look. "You know, the Catholic church is very forgiving. And once you get over this Baptist stuff, I'm sure they'll take you right back."

Take me back? What is she talking about? I wasn't the wayward one here – she was!

"Well," I replied, trying to be gentle, "I don't think I'll be going back THERE again. I mean, they don't even read the bible at that church!" My haughty holy attitude wasn't winning any points here. I didn't know what to say. Mom wasn't happy. Dad wasn't happy. The tension was so thick I felt like I might choke. So we just stood there being unhappy for several minutes until I mumbled some excuse about having to go do something, and she went back to her dishes and I secluded myself in my room.

It was days before they would talk to me again. And it would be years before they believed I was really converted. Mom kept saying, "Every Sunday, I leave a little room in the pew for you at church." And at the dinner table I'd say, "You know, there's a lot of people at our church who used to be Catholics." Then another day my dad would say, "Two Baptists became converts at church today. They're taking classes and becoming real Catholics now." It was a mess. Nobody ever won. I went my way; they went theirs. And so it still stands today.

Chapter 27:   The Big Question

OK, now, nobody's home. We're in my parent's front room. Kellie is in the big brown chair across the room from me. She's wearing one of her "sack dresses", which is like overalls with a shirt underneath. She's sitting there, smiling quietly, looking over expectantly as I try to stay calm. I was sitting on our couch, staring at the bright orange 1970's carpet (gosh, I hated that ugly thing!) trying to gather some courage. Thoughts raced through my mind. I had to do this now. I knew I wanted to. But what would she say? How would she react? Does she know why I'm over here sweating blood? Would she be surprised? Would she be offended? Hmph. I doubted that. Would she be shocked? Would she jump up, clutch her heart and fall to the floor as her convulsing body spewed spittle onto the big orange headache-maker?

OK, OK, I don't need to be thinking about her convulsing body right now.

I really was fond of Kellie. I had never felt so totally connected with someone before, not even as a child when two kids can talk honestly with each other, before you grow up and learn how to use big words & hide behind complex sentences that go on forever and never seem to end because you have to say a bunch of big enormous gargantuan gigantic words to make sure the other person understands because they're not really listening to you, they're listening to your words and trying to interpret when all you really need when you're a kid is a few simple phrases and it's totally obvious because it's simple, and it still is really, but people are just afraid to let other people in or trust their instinct and intuition so they wouldn't have to drone on and on, saying basically nothing but feeling safe because they have something to do which is move their mouth and make fairly intelligible sounds that turn into words that bounce off the other grown-up's ears while a very little gets through. Good thing I'm not like that.

We had done everything right so far. We were just friends for a long time, talking together for hours, especially over the phone. I'd lay in bed with the phone between my ear and pillow, silently listening to her sweet voice, imagining being with her and how great it would be some day to not have to be quiet so my parents can't hear. We spent a lot of time in my bedroom, just talking or listening to music. We hadn't even kissed until long after David was born. The first time was in my bedroom. I had a microphone left over from my heavy-metal band (or pathetic attempt of one), and Kellie was doing silly things with it, talking babyish & just being cute. She used to like to hear herself over the speakers. I was teasing her & tried to get the microphone away from her, and we just kind of froze there, staring at each other. We lost all sense of time as our lips drifted ever so slowly together. It's the kind of thing you read about in a novel. I couldn't speak. I couldn't move. I was caught in Kellie's tractor beam of love.

There were a lot of things that brought us close together. She was gorgeous, of course, and available, and easy to talk to, and pretty, and had a very nice voice, and she didn't look too bad either, or did I say that already? But what brought me to the point of wiping the sweat off my hands in nervous anticipation there in the living room was something else. I'd met good-looking girls before. Not many, mind you. I wasn't what you'd call a chick magnet by any means; more like a beauty repellant. But I just got to where I wanted to be with her forever, and raise a family together, and never, ever have to be without her again. It drove me nuts to have to leave her at her dad's house at night. That's probably why I'd go straight home, call her & talk for hours more.

It was also Kellie's view of family that won me over. People these days, they get married for the wrong reasons. They want security, or money, or they just "feel like it." And if it doesn't work out, just call a lawyer. But that's not what I heard from Kellie. She wanted a family; she wanted to stay with someone forever, no matter what. She felt like God's plan was for the woman to be a keeper at home, and be there to help her husband. She wanted to stay home and raise her child; not throw him in daycare & hope for the best. It even bothered her when her mom watched the little guy. Bothered me, too. I wanted to take Kellie and her little baby away, take charge, be a man & provide for these guys. Not just a friend. Not even a boyfriend. In fact, I was secretly hoping I'd be the first one that he called "Daddy."

Whew, was it getting hot in here? My heart felt like it was going to jump out of my chest. My head felt tingly. I couldn't feel my feet. My hands were shaking. I clutched them together tightly to make them stop.

I thought, I'd better do this before I lose what little nerve I've mustered up. Take a deep breath. Try to sound calm. Be a man. Do it now. Just do it.

"Kellie, I have a question for you," I stammered. My voice quivered slightly. I hoped she didn't notice.

"Yes?" she replied expectantly. She knew something was up. I could tell.

OK, Mark, do this thing right. Remember the Nike commercial. Just do it. Remember why you're doing this. Remember how much you love her. Remember the Alamo. Remember anything, just move, dadgumit.

I took one last gulp of air, swallowed, and rose to my feet. I felt like I was watching myself move as I glided across the room and bent down on one knee. I took her hand as her eyes got so wide I thought her eyeballs would pop out. I didn't even notice that my pulse was now over a thousand beats per minute and my lungs had collapsed.

Somehow, I managed the words, "Kellie, will you marry me?"

My heart stopped. My breathing stopped. My brain got hung up like a Windows 95 computer as I froze in suspended animation. Kellie smiled a coy little grin. "I don't know, Mark." She was laughing nervously from the shock. "Mark, I don't know."

"I'll take real good care of you," I replied emphatically. "I'll never hurt you ever, and I'll never ever leave you, and I'll be good to you & buy you stuff." My heart rate rose another 50 percent. "I'll take care of you forever," I added, as the heartbeat in my ear rose to a deafening roar.

Kellie was smiling as a tear appeared in her eye.

"Oh, you can take all the time you need!" I offered. "You don't have to decide right now. It's OK if you need some time."

Kellie looked at me thoughtfully. Then she said those words I was so desperate to hear. "OK. Yes."

"You're sure? You don't need to think about it? Because this is a big decision, and I don't want you to…"

"No, I'm sure," she interrupted with a smile. She gave my hand a squeeze.

"Really?" Oh, the relief! Oh, the relief! I'll say it again. Oh, the relief! I couldn't believe it. She nodded. I hugged her. I stroked her hair as I squeezed her shoulders and promised, "I'll be a real good husband, you'll see. I'll take real good care of you, and David too, and we won't ever have to be apart again. Never, ever again."

I closed my eyes and started to cry a little myself, as we sat there, embracing together on my dad's big brown chair. I rocked her back & forth gently as I thought, This is going to be great. New faith. New wife. A whole new life! We're going to be together forever now, and no one will ever take us apart again.

I knew it was a tough road ahead, but I also knew Jesus was there to travel it with us; to forgive us when we messed up, to bless us when we didn't deserve it, and to carry us when we could no longer walk.

With Jesus on our side, everything is going to be different now, I thought to myself. Everything is going to be great. I could just imagine my new wife and me, together in our new home. She'd be in the kitchen, handing me my breakfast plate, smiling sweetly at our new baby as he gooed and gawed in his little high chair. No more being alone and depressed. No more waiting to see her only after work or on weekends. That sweet, lovely creature was going to be all mine, and we would be blissfully happy together, 24/7. It was going to be a great, great life.

Chapter 28:   When Reality Kicks In

I approached the apartment with a bit of queasiness in my stomach. I knew what probably lay on the other side of that door. I had seen it many times. People sometimes go their whole lives without experiencing the absolute mayhem and destruction that awaited me.

I'd gotten the call over two hours ago, then, mysteriously, not a word. I paused to gather my strength before the door to my 1973 Plymouth Valiant squeaked open. I let out a sigh. OK, I have to be prepared for anything. I will not be shocked. No, not this time. I will be brave.

I let out a sigh as I faced the building. It was an older apartment complex, right in the heart of Pasadena, Texas. The roof was rotting. The windows were cracked. The paint was peeling. It was a far cry from the ritzy mansions on the other side of the city. Places that had fresh paint, a gate you have to go through to get in with a little security card, sidewalks that were flat with almost no grass growing in the cracks, swimming pools, and most of all, other tenants. Oh, there were some other people around, but they didn't venture to this end of the complex. No, we had to get the last building next to the 6-foot chain link fence that separated us from the overgrown, untended lot that no human had been in for at least a century. But worse than what it looked like outside, was my imagination of what laid wait behind that green/gray/sortof brown front door.

I shook my head, trying to spin out the pictures in my brain. I can do this. It can't be worse than last time, can it? I grabbed my briefcase from the back seat, which still felt awkward in my hand. I hadn't quite gotten into this go-to-work-everyday, be-a-grownup thing, but I knew a briefcase was an important part of it. All my life, my dad's carried one back & forth to work, every day. It tells the world you're important. It's black, it's plastic, it's tough. It's a Samsonite, for cryin' out loud. That's nearly as strong as God. I pushed the car door shut, and after the glass stopped rattling, I clenched my jaw and carried that badge of brawn right across the pavement up to the front door, took a deep breath, and opened it up.

The light from the outside beamed over my shoulder as the door swung slowly open, illuminating the path of terror I knew I must travel. The darkness inside gave a heaviness to the air that was only partially mitigated by the advancing sunlight behind me. I could feel my forehead wrinkle as I assessed the situation. There were toys everywhere. Lego blocks. Tinker toys. What used to be a fully assembled couch now had its members placed sporadically about the room. In the kitchen I could see what few dishes we had, spilling out over the counter and over the bar onto the kitchen table. The high chair sat in the corner, its tray tossed to the side onto the table, revealing a residue of what looked like jelly, chocolate and something red.

Candy wrappers littered the carpet in a path from the front room down the hallway.

"Kellie?" I timidly asked. "Are you OK?" There was no answer. Closing the door softly, I navigated around the fallen plastic slide, through the ocean of Ninja Turtles, scarcely finding a foothold amongst all the dingdong wrappers and dirty diapers. I set my briefcase down in the kitchen, next to the soup cans that had dribbled off the pantry shelves. As I made my way into the bedroom area, I could feel hundreds of little cheerios, making a popping noise as they were crushed beneath my massive imitation-leather work shoes.

As I reached the doorway, I peered around the corner, and there she was. Kellie's body was limp, hunched over a coverless pillow on the floor, still poised in a reaching position with her fingertips just inches away from the container of baby powder. A half-eaten bag of Hershey's Kisses lay by her side. Her clothes were littered with crumbs and stains like shrapnel. The TV was silently flashing out a cartoon, also on the floor, with one rabbit ear drooping down and the other staunchly upright, short and broken. Its light danced across my son's face, as he lay motionless, wearing only a diaper & nestled amidst plastic wrappers, baby wipes, and aluminum Kiss wrappers. Around him, the blast radius extended about 6 feet in each direction. There were diapers. There were wipes. The carpet lay peppered with cereal and cookie crumbs as far as the eye could see. Clothes lay strewn across the area like the leaves of an Oak in late Fall. The closet doors were all open, their contents spilling out like great tongues of the Closet Beast. And above the whole scene rose a smell. A smell so unique, so different, yet so ordinary and familiar. A smell comprised of not one, but many parts. Poop. Baby wipes. Chocolate. Snot. Soap. And what was that? Just a touch of corn. Must have been some chips in there somewhere.

My little family looked so peaceful, sleeping there, not even aware that I'd come home. Yet, I could see everywhere around me the evidence of that day's struggles. I slid against the wall and sat down with a sigh, trying not to tip over the half-eaten box of Lucky Charms. I knew what her day had been like. I think the best hint I got was when she was screaming to me over the phone earlier. What was it she said again? Something about, He's driving me crazy, I can't take it any more, Can't you come home now, What am I going to do, Stop it David!, Oh, no! I gotta go, <click>. After that, silence. I knew then that I'd find this when I got home. I knew she'd been having a tough time. The rest of the story was all too plain to see. The fussing, the bribing, the screaming, the eating, the chasing, then finally, exhaustion and collapse.

Well, I thought to myself, here I am. On my own, with my new wife, new baby, sitting in my very own apartment, surrounded by the contents of the first two aisles of the grocery store. I sat there for a few minutes, just taking in the scene. I could hear cars & trucks as they zoomed on the beltway in the distance. A few birds chirped from the empty lot net door. And I could just barely hear an argument in Spanish drifting in from the other end of the complex. This was my new home now, and the start of a whole new life. I closed my eyes and thanked God for these two sleeping angels. It would be a couple of hours before either of them stirred from their sugar-induced coma. I opened my eyes, smiled, took up the box of Lucky Charms and walked into the living room.

God is good, isn't He?

www.ingramcontent.com/pod-product-compliance
Lightning Source LLC
Chambersburg PA
CBHW052012090426
42741CB00008B/1661